There Are *Alligators* in Our Sewers and Other American Credos

Books by Paul Dickson

THINK TANKS
THE GREAT AMERICAN ICE CREAM BOOK
THE FUTURE OF THE WORKPLACE
THE ELECTRONIC BATTLEFIELD
THE MATURE PERSON'S GUIDE TO KITES, YO-YOS,
    FRISBEES, AND OTHER CHILDLIKE DIVERSIONS
OUT OF THIS WORLD: AMERICAN SPACE PHOTOGRAPHY
THE FUTURE FILE
CHOW: A COOK'S TOUR OF MILITARY FOOD
THE OFFICIAL RULES
THE OFFICIAL EXPLANATIONS
TOASTS
WORDS

Books by Joseph C. Goulden

THE CURTIS CAPER
MONOPOLY
TRUTH IS THE FIRST CASUALTY
THE MONEY-GIVERS
THE SUPERLAWYERS
MEANY: A BIOGRAPHY
THE BENCHWARMERS
THE BEST YEARS
MENCKEN'S LAST CAMPAIGN:
    H. L. MENCKEN ON THE 1948 ELECTIONS *(Editor)*
THE MILLION DOLLAR LAWYERS
KOREA: THE UNTOLD STORY OF THE WAR
LABOR'S LAST ANGRY MAN: A BIOGRAPHY OF JERRY WURF

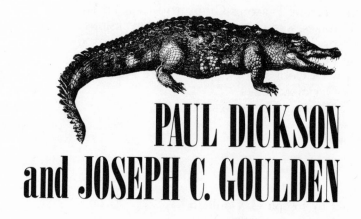

PAUL DICKSON
and JOSEPH C. GOULDEN

Illustrated by R. J. SHAY

There Are *Alligators* in Our Sewers and Other American Credos

DELACORTE PRESS/NEW YORK

Published by
Delacorte Press
1 Dag Hammarskjold Plaza
New York, N.Y. 10017

Acknowledgment is made for permission to reprint ten items from pp. 185–187, 205–207 by Burton Rascoe in MORROW'S ALMANACK AND EVERY-DAY BOOK FOR 1930 edited by Thayer Hobson. Copyright 1929 by William Morrow & Company, Inc. By permission of the publisher.

Manufactured in the United States of America

First printing

Designed by Giorgetta Bell McRee

LIBRARY OF CONGRESS CATALOGING IN PUBLICATION DATA

Dickson, Paul.
There are alligators in our sewers and other American credos.

Bibliography: p.
Includes index.
1. Folklore—United States.   2. Urban folklore—United States.
3. Superstition—United States.
I. Goulden, Joseph C.   II. Title.
GR105.D53 1983   398'.0973   82–17946
ISBN 0–440–08882–8

To the unnamed *Time* editor who wrote this
for the September 28, 1970, issue of the magazine:

In 1920, Satirists H. L. Mencken and George Jean Nathan published a
book called *The American Credo*. It contained a chrestomathy of
shibboleths, prejudices, common beliefs and unexamined truisms held sacred
by millions—"That it snowed every Christmas down to fifteen years ago,"
for example, or "that oysters are a great aphrodisiac." The *Credo* badly
needs updating.

TERMS

Credo is Latin for "I believe." As an English word it originally referred to religious creeds, such as the Apostles' Creed, but then came to mean any belief or creed. Mainly due to the influence of H. L. Mencken and George Jean Nathan and their book *The American Credo,* it has taken on a new meaning in the twentieth century. Today it commonly refers to a widely held belief or piece of conventional wisdom which is partially, predominantly, or totally wrong. In this book we deal exclusively with this type of credo.

These wrongheaded credos naturally break down into two basic species. First, there are the *specific credos:* bits of silliness that must be apocryphal in origin—beliefs about reptiles in sewers and admirals being unable to navigate rowboats. Secondly, there is the *philosophical credo:* a belief with a genuine element of truth to it, but one that has become so clichéd and overapplied that it now exhibits a genuine element of falsehood. Examples: that there are two sides to every question, or that you can discipline your mind. (If you've just caught yourself saying, "What? of course that's true!"—you've been suckered in by another credo.) This collection concentrates on the former, but is salted with some of the latter.

The twentieth-century American credo also has a first cousin that any self-respecting credo collector cannot resist accumulating. It is the modern fable—or what folklorists call the urban folktale—and it is essentially a credo that has been turned into a story. The authors proudly exhibit their fable collection along with their credos.

CONTENTS

PREFACE
After H. L. Mencken

"The trouble with most folks isn't so much their ignorance, as knowing so many things that ain't so."
—**Josh Billings**

"Deep down in every man there is a body of congenital attitudes, a corpus of ineradicable doctrines and ways of thinking, that determines his reactions to his ideational environment as surely as his physical activity is determined by the length of his *tibiae* and the capacity of his lungs."
—**H. L. Mencken** and **George Jean Nathan**,
The American Credo, 1920

From the first stirrings of childhood the American acquires an ever-thickening encrustation of ideas, beliefs, and dogma that makes life all the simpler. Tribal truths pass to him from his elders and his contemporaries, to be assimilated into common acceptances, an intellectual shorthand that enables him to pass through life with a minimum of mental effort. What, for instance, does one really need to know about dogs save that a canine who wags his tail when barking is not a menace? Or that the primary function of carrots is to strengthen one's eyesight? Or that the consumption of fish benefits the brain? Specialists in zoology, nutrition, and neurology perhaps will seek a bit more detail; the layman cares to know no more.

That much of what passes for "knowledge" in America is rank nonsense is of no great importance. The progress of mankind is oiled by perceptions, not realities. That the general populace treats a notion as truth gives it a momentum and a life of its own. Indeed, major segments of our society survive because of this principle. What politician dares introduce a truly new idea to the electorate? Consider the Democratic party. For two decades its office seekers of any denomination, from alderman to President, merely had to bellow "Herbert Hoover" from time to time, code words that reminded the electorate of the Depression, and the person responsible for it. The Republicans, equally sharp on the rules of play, needed only to mutter "Alger Hiss" and "Who lost China?" to wiggle their way back to the front of the line.

In each of these instances the parties relied upon a "credo"—the willingness of Americans to accept a proposition as fact, without cumbersome footnotes and explanations. The credo thus has a double utility: the people who employ it need go no further than a phrase, a wink and a nod; the people who hear it are conditioned to accept what is offered.

That Americans have been subjected to an "information explosion" the last decade verily is a credo unto itself. Assuredly the quantity of offered information has increased dramatically. Satellite television transmissions permit us to witness the assassination of the president of Egypt in 1981 within an hour after the event. When Napoleon's army floundered in Egypt in 1798, news of the disaster did not reach Paris for months. Our newsstands offer magazines on every "specialty" from bathroom design to the techniques of placer mining. Yet how much of

Sullivan. The assassinations, and the plot-cults attendant to them. *Incredulous* survives only as a word found in the dictionary.

Thus we have grafted onto the homilies of the past the new nuttiness of the present. Peasants once fell prostrate at the sight of an eclipse of the sun, bellowing to the deities for salvation, convinced that a supernatural being was about to snatch them off the earth. Their lineal descendants—that is to say, we—have progressed to a belief in extraplanetary spaceships that prowl the backwoods by night, collecting herdsmen and beautiful girls, and perhaps indulging in blood sacrifices of livestock as well. That "evidence" of such happenings is skimpy is laid to "the government," which conceals "fact" lest the populace panic.

Yet this sort of nonsense does have social utility. One of the authors once listened, with marked interest, to the ideas propounded by persons who telephoned a late-night radio talk show. The subject at hand happened to be the military, and the callers advanced some most conspiratorial views of contemporary history: that General Douglas MacArthur and Marshal Georgi Zhukov, the Red Army commander, "planned" the Korean War during a secret meeting in Thailand in 1947; and that a "Russian general at the United Nations" directed overall American military strategy in the Korean War. "This is kind of far-out stuff," the author remarked to the moderator, who replied, "Yeah, but at least listening to the radio keeps them off the street. Would you rather have them running around at this time of night?" No. The offsetting mischief, however, is that a listener elsewhere hears a snatch of this gabble, and stores it away as truth—because, after all, does not the Federal Communications Commission have laws against false information being disseminated over the radio?

The amount of evidence required to substantiate the validity of a credo is a free-floating variable. For example, "Bad airplane accidents always occur in threes." If there is a major airline crash, adherents to the "threes credo" keep a watch on the newspapers the following days. In all probability they'll read about a second crash in the Far West, and of another in South America. Thus the "threes credo" is substantiated. Or news of the jailing of a minister on morals charges reinforces the conviction that much naughtiness is performed under the guise of theology, statistical evidence to the contrary notwithstanding.

That the modern myths have established themselves as an integral part of American folklore is recognized by no less a cultural barometer than Hollywood. During the 1960s there were murmurings from the nut fringe that the space shots and moon walks never occurred; that in actuality all these events were staged on remote sites in the Nevada desert. ("Look at any road map. See these vast areas that are marked 'military reservations'? That's where it happened.") In 1978 Hollywood put a variation of this canard onto film in *Capricorn One,* in which O. J. Simpson, Hal Holbrook, and James Brolin played bogus astronauts. *Capricorn* was quickly followed by *The Formula,* with George C. Scott and Marlon Brando feuding over the secret to cheap oil being kept off the market by evil oil companies; *Alligator,* about those reptiles prowling the New York City sewers; and *Hangar 18,* the story of the crashed UFO and the frozen bodies found thereon being stored at Wright-Patterson Air Force Base in Ohio. Scott Morris, who watches unconfirmed rumors for *OMNI* magazine, sees a vast potential for related movies: "First out will be *Scallop!* about a ruthless restaurateur who serves cut-out shark or skate to unsuspecting customers who have ordered shellfish."

One saving grace for many of the credos is that they are laced with a strong tot of fun. One of the hoariest culinary stories involves the overbearing rich matron who demands that a swank hotel sell her the secret recipe for "red velvet cake." (This has happened at such hostelries as the Waldorf-Astoria in New York, the Fairmont in San Francisco, and the Roosevelt in New Orleans.) For five hundred dollars the chef finally relents. The secret: add a half cup of red food coloring to a package of regular cake mix. The Waldorf management stopped trying to deny the story decades ago (the hotel has never served red velvet cake or any approximation); there are times when one chooses to shut up and enjoy the story along with everyone else. And, again, credos can be used to state perceptions of bitter reality. James Davis, a black correspondent and sometime collector of credos, remembers a legend told to him "by old folks when I was growing up: that if NASA ever found black folks elsewhere in the universe, this would bring space exploration to a halt."

We offer *There are Alligators . . .* as a cultural way station; as an informal compilation of some of the beliefs, major and minor, that fuel our nation as the 1980s commence. Whether a credo is bogus or genuine is irrelevant: these are the things being said (and repeated) on America's streets, front pages, and airwaves. Were it possible for a sociologist or cultural anthropologist to trace each to its origin, assuredly a kernel of original truth might be found at the site.

The authors, both Mencken enthusiasts, bow with gratitude toward *The American Credo,* compiled and published by H. L. Mencken and George Jean Nathan in 1920. (These partners later split, for irrelevant reasons, and the latter carried on the credos work with two subsequent volumes issued later in the 1920s.) Our first contribution to contemporary credos was published in *The Washingtonian* magazine in July 1979. Within weeks our modest effort was heralded throughout the Republic, with the article either reprinted or commented upon by such august journals as the *Chicago Tribune,* the *Dallas Morning News,* the Des Moines *Register, The Bulletin* of Philadelphia, and the *St. Louis Post-Dispatch.* As a means of bringing scientific order to further research, the authors created the Center for Research into Epigrammatic Dogmatic Observations (CREDO), with international headquarters at Post Office Box 80, Garrett Park, Maryland 20896. (Among the organizations that did not give support to CREDO were the National Endowment for the Humanities, the Rockefeller Foundation, and the Page County, Virginia, Center for the Support of Creative Arts.) Contributions of credos were solicited from a wide range of persons, and their kindness to the authors is more formally acknowledged at the end of the book.

CREDO intends to continue the compilation of credos, in the interest of the advancement of our contemporary culture. Persons desirous of adding their own favorite credos to the existing body of knowledge are cordially invited to communicate with the authors at the CREDO address listed above.

Animals

- That the Smithsonian is in possession of the remains of several American animals of fantastic proportions and attributes, but that they are hidden from public view and their presence denied because they do not jibe with present-day scientific theory. (For instance the great gowrow, which was shipped to the museum in 1897 by a traveling salesman from Arkansas. It was heavily scaled, tusked, hornbacked, and twenty feet long.)

- That giant alligators thrive in the sewer systems of our major cities as a consequence of people having bought baby alligators in Florida, then having tired of them and finally flushed them down their toilets.

(In his book *World Beneath the City* Robert Daley reported on an interview with former New York Commissioner of Sewers Teddy May, who said that men in his department spotted two-foot-long alligators in the city's sewers in 1935. It was first assumed that the men had been drinking, but further investigation confirmed the alligators. May said that with the aid of poison and .22 rifles they were wiped out by 1937.

This is a clear case of a belief that has a modicum of truth to it,

That giant alligators thrive in the sewer systems of our major cities as a consequence of people buying baby alligators in Florida, tiring of them, and finally flushing them down their toilets.

although that truth is a far cry from the Cadillac-sized beasts of legend.)

- That bats are drawn to the hair on the human head and will become tangled therein.
- That bears often hug their human victims to death.
- That a bee pays for the act of stinging a human by dying.
- That birds only sing at sunset and dawn.
- That bulls are infuriated by the color red.
- That camels store water in their humps.
- That cats are smarter than dogs but that dogs have better personalities.
- That any cat, given the opportunity, will hover over the crib of a baby and suck its breath until it dies.
- That chameleons are able to change color depending on the background they are in front of. Those which we have encountered which do not turn plaid in front of a sport shirt are obviously either defective or some other kind of lizard.
- That centipedes have one hundred legs.
- That cockroaches can survive in any environment, which is why they are routinely discovered in mine shafts, volcano mouths, orbiting spacecraft, and Manhattan apartments.
- That dinosaurs were the bane of cavemen.

(Despite the fact that the interval between the last dinosaur and the first man was at least 60 million years, this myth is still strong, no doubt aided by countless Hollywood films in which the beasts bedevil cave dwellers.)

- That a dog senses the death of its master even though they are separated by many miles.
- That dogs are able to judge human character. ("Puzzy likes you, he knows you are honest and wouldn't be cruel to him.") Ditto for cats. ("Princess never ever sits in a stranger's lap. You must be a fine and caring person.")

That cockroaches can survive in any environment, which is why they are routinely discovered in mine shafts, volcano mouths, orbiting spacecraft, and Manhattan apartments.

- That you can't teach an old dog new tricks.
- That barking dogs don't bite.
- That you should never allow a strange dog to know that you are afraid.

- That dogs frequently detect fires and bark in such a way as to warn humans of the danger.
- That it is just a matter of time until humans and dolphins find a way to communicate. At that time the dolphin will tell us all sorts of remarkable things, including, perhaps, the full story of Atlantis. (When this assertion is made, it is always stated in terms of what the dolphins will tell us, rather than what we'll tell them. Will we read to them from the latest issue of *People* or show them the latest episode of *CHiPs?*)
- That elephants head for an immense graveyard when it is time for them to die. The location of this treasury of ivory has long eluded human discovery. Elephants recall the location of the graveyard only in their final hours.
- That elephants are afraid of mice.
- That goats eat shoes and tin cans.
- That lemmings commit mass suicide by herding themselves into the ocean.
- That it does not bother or pain a lobster to be cooked alive. Nor, for that matter, does it hurt a cow when it's branded.
- That mice prefer cheese to all other foods.
- That large octopuses can and do strangle humans.
- That ostriches hide their heads in the sand.
- That owls and cats can see in total darkness.
- That pigeons have a natural affinity for statues.
- That no one has ever seen a baby pigeon, despite years of observation of their nesting places with telephoto lenses.
- That porcupines are able to shoot their quills when aroused.
- That the proper way to pick up a rabbit is by its ears.
- That rats leave a sinking ship.
- That if you give enough of anything to a laboratory rat it will get cancer.

That it does not bother or pain a lobster to be cooked alive.

- That snakes paralyze their intended victims with a hypnotic stare.
- That whales spout water.
- That if you cut a worm in half it will grow into two worms. (Sometimes, depending upon the type of worm. But after such a division, a worm loses much of its interest in life and dies without further ingestion or reproduction.)

The Arts

- That all great artists are thin (presumably because of the suffering they have had to endure).
- That if it were not for *The Nutcracker* and *Swan Lake,* American ballet would have long ago ceased to exist.
- That while the total fraud inherent in modern abstract art is immediately obvious to the man on the street, it is totally missed by the critics, museum curators, and wealthy patrons of the arts.
- That the world envisioned in the paintings of Norman Rockwell was a real one, but a world that has now largely disappeared.
- That most furniture sold as antiques in Maine, New Hampshire, upstate New York, Massachusetts, and/or Vermont actually was made the previous winter and aged by using it in homes of clumsy people.
- That some of the finest, most important, and sensitive photographs ever taken were made by amateurs with box cameras. That a young child or old man fishing with crude equipment and worms will always reach his limit before a man with the latest and most expensive gear. That if the scribblings of toddlers were framed and hung on the

That while the total fraud inherent in modern abstract art is immediately obvious to the man on the street, it is totally missed by the critics, museum curators, and wealthy patrons of the arts.

walls of the appropriate galleries, they would sell for a small fortune and be proclaimed as the last word in abstract expressionism.

- That there is a code associated with the statues of military heroes. If all four of the horse's feet are on the ground, it means that the general survived the war. If one foot is off the ground, it means that he was wounded, and two feet off the ground symbolizes death on the battlefield.
- That if you prowl around flea markets and garage sales long enough, you'll eventually find some unrecognized treasure at a ridiculously low price.
- That the experts come to these sales at the crack of dawn and haul away the good stuff, which is why you never find any yourself.
- That in order for a writer, poet, or artist to achieve greatness, he or she must be either neurotic or possessed of a fatal flaw.
- That people no longer know how to dance.

Business

- That it is un-American not to pad your expense account.
- That someone somewhere higher up in the organization really knows what's going on, and will be competent to save us when the shit hits the fan.

- That seashore building lots sold by mail solicitations are three or more feet beneath water; that "vacation-home sites" similarly marketed in the West are inaccessible patches of desert.
- That if an ad appears that contains an incorrectly low price, the advertiser must sell the item in question for that low price.
- That it pays to advertise.
- That renegade advertisers flash invisible-to-the-eye, but subconsciously perceived, messages to television viewers during commercials and programs alike.
- That there is a little-known federal law that prohibits retailers from announcing overly low low-sale prices in print advertisements or over the air. The merchant will announce his prices are "so low we can't mention them!"
- That White Rock's "Lady of the Lake" is still seen occasionally by teen-aged couples parking on summer nights.
- That if the Ford Motor Company would manufacture Model A's again, they would become the biggest best sellers in auto history; that most of what Detroit produces today are lemons.
- That if all American corporate presidents spent a year or so in Japan, studying superior management techniques, our economy would right itself within two or three years.
- That the phone company has a secret monitoring center out in St. Louis—or maybe it's Minneapolis—where every phone conversation made in the U.S. is recorded on computers. These tapes are routinely given to the FBI, the CIA, and bill-collection agencies.
- That clicking or other noise on your phone line is a strong indication some scoundrel is tapping it.

(Unlikely, given technological advances of the past two decades.)
- That it is possible to devise better things for better living through chemistry.

- That the name of the retail chain of E. J. Korvette was short for Eight Jewish Korean War Veterans.

(Korvette founder Eugene Ferkauf explained in his book *Going into Business* that the E. was for his first name, the J. was for that of associate and pal, Joe Swillenberg; and the Korvette was picked because it has a "euphonious ring." He got it from the name of the Canadian war vessel corvette and changed the C to a K when he found it illegal to register the name of a naval class identity.)

- That copulating polar bears and the like are drawn into the photographs of drinks in liquor ads to help sell the product. Although hard to find with the naked eye, these sexual images work on us subliminally.

- That you should buy razor blades during the World Series (or during other times when the companies that make them sponsor advertising blitzes), as they are purposely made sharper then, so that anyone trying them for the first time will be so amazed and impressed that he will become a lifetime customer.

- That owners of small businesses spend all of their time filling out forms devised by federal bureaucrats.

- That no shortages are real: somewhere off both coasts are ships holding great quantities of crude oil, sirloin steak, and cotton bales, to drive up the prices.

- That electric utilities periodically overload their lines to burn out light bulbs. Some go out at once, others survive a few hours. But if one light bulb burns out, two to three others will follow within a day. The manufacturers of bulbs pay the utilities to perform this service, because under normal circumstances the bulbs would last for years.

- Also, that the same parties have long conspired to prevent the appearance of a truly long-lasting "lifetime" electric light bulb—something which has been technically possible for decades.

• That if one writes a letter of complaint about certain products, the response will be to get a case of that product in compensation.

• That all gasoline is the same, and tanker trucks from a number of companies routinely line up to be supplied from a common source.

• That every Tuesday or so a malcontent assembly-line worker puts a handful of gravel into the hubcap of a new Cadillac, along with a note intended to be found weeks later that reads, "So you finally found the rattle, you rich SOB!"

• That people who live in towns with horrible industrial odors not only learn to live with the smell but invariably tell outsiders who mention it, "That's the smell of money."

• That any crowd at an auction contains at least three shills whose duty is to bid up prices for the item you really want. They stand in separate parts of the room and do not acknowledge that they know one another or the auctioneer.

• That if it weren't for the excesses of big labor, big business, and big government, there would be no inflation.

• That a Rolls-Royce engine is sealed when the car leaves the factory and must not be touched by any mechanic save an expert dispatched from Great Britain. If a Rolls-Royce breaks down anytime during its life warranty, the manufacturer will fly a mechanic to the owner's location, wherever it may be, to make the repairs.

• That falling hemlines on women's fashions are a forewarning of financial panics; that shorter skirts mean go-go soars in the Dow Jones industrial average.

• That if a team that was a member of the original National Football League (before expansion to include several American Football League teams) wins the Super Bowl, the stock market will rise during the year.

(Since 1967, when the first Super Bowl was played, this has been a "very accurate" indicator, according to an article in the Chicago Sun-

Times. As of this writing, 1982 looks like a good year to invest because the 49ers won the Super Bowl a few weeks ago.)

WARNING! DANGER ZONE! WARNING!

The following Credos and Rumors are ABSOLUTELY UNTRUE and have already caused great damage to those involved. Use only as examples of how WRONGHEADED rumors can get.

Anyone quoting them as true and referring to the fact that they read them in this book will be subject to the following CURSE: FOR ALL ETERNITY YOUR READING WILL BE RESTRICTED TO NATIONAL TABLOIDS FOUND IN SUPERMARKET CHECK-OUT LANES.

· · · **THE MANAGEMENT** · · ·

- That Dr Pepper is made from prune juice, that Pepperidge Farm pretzels contain lye, and that a woman once found a dead mouse in a bottle of Coca-Cola, sued for a million dollars, and won.
- That several months before Gillette puts a new razor blade on the market it deliberately lowers the quality of the current quality line. A man who has been comfortable shaving with a Gillette platinum finds that it drags and cuts. So he buys the Super-Platinum, and is happy. In fact, the Super-Platinum is no better than the "Blue Blade" marketed during the 1940s.
- That spider eggs have been found in Bubble Yum, McDonald's hamburgers have been beefed up with ground worms, and Pop Rocks have exploded in kids' stomachs. That Teflon-contaminated cigarettes have killed, welders have been blown into tiny pieces because they carried butane lighters in their pockets, and the secret of a popular cigarette filter is that it uses ground glass. That Girl Scout Cookies, along

with other popular products, are laced with THC or hashish and that consumers routinely discover Kentucky-fried rats, char-broiled fingers, and worse in fast-food restaurants. That the Reverend Moon and/or devil worshipers have taken control of Procter & Gamble . . .

(Collectively, these untruisms have cost the companies involved a quadruple king's ransom running campaigns to dispel them. Squibb, which owns Bubble Yum, spent more than one hundred thousand dollars trying to kill the spider-egg falsehood, and Pepperidge Farm was compelled to put one of its top executives on the television talk-show circuit to spike the lye lie by eating pretzels in front of the camera.)

(For years Procter & Gamble patiently noted that its famed man-in-the-moon corporate logo had evolved over decades and contained no secret satanic meanings. Nonetheless, fundamentalist preachers and peddlers of rival sundries persisted in spreading the "satan runs P&G" rumor. In the summer of 1982 the corporation sued more than half a dozen persons it accused of perpetuating the myth. At one time P&G was receiving an incredible 12,000 written queries monthly about the canard.)

•   That when a person turns fifty-seven, he can write to the Heinz food company and get a free carton of Heinz products.

(Actually this was true until the 1950s, according to Rudy Maxa in his *Washington Post* column for March 21, 1982.)

Children

- That children suffer from growing pains.
- That making a child walk too early will give him bowed legs.
- That children should always wear clean underwear just in case they are involved in an accident and have to be undressed in the hospital.
- That children who attend Catholic parochial school are more given to swearing and telling dirty jokes than public school kids.
- That video games improve a child's eye-hand coordination.
- That political terrorists come from wealthy parents.
- That prodigies start off with a bang but soon peter out.
- That most boys who grow up to amount to something have had newspaper routes and belonged to the Boy Scouts.
- That the proper college fraternity gives a young man an immeasurable boost up the ladder of success. That military service exerts a calming influence on young men.
- That a child born in the summer will tend to be smarter than one born during any other season.

(This belief has been so widespread that studies were conducted to see if it had any validity. The answer, as reported in the *British Medical Journal* for March 4, 1944, is that it is untrue.)

That most boys who grow up to amount to something have had newspaper routes and belonged to the Boy Scouts.

- That children of right-wing parents grow up to flame as liberals and vice versa.
- That children with high IQs tend to be sicklier and not as well adjusted as those with normal or low IQs. The lower-IQ kids will grow up to be more successful in their jobs and marriages.

(All of this is absolutely false, according to Lewis Terman, a Stanford psychologist who has studied children with higher IQs.)

- That children always grow taller than their parents.
- That the youngest child is always spoiled and, consequently, worthless.
- That daughters tend to resemble their mothers, after sufficient time.
- That children of large families are more "normal" than children of small families.
- That daughters like their dads best and vice versa.
- That if a nine-year-old boy digs a hole through the earth from any location in the United States, he will emerge on the outskirts of Peking, China.
- That the offspring of first cousins are likely to be feebleminded.
- That powerful families go to hell in the third generation of power.

SMALL BOY CREDOS

- That the only suitable way to break in a new catcher's mitt is to fit a baseball into the desired "pocket," and bind the mitt tightly with leather thongs for several days. The resultant pocket will be permanent and enable the small boy to perform on a par with Johnny Bench or Yogi Berra.

•   That no pocket knife with less than seven blades is worth carrying around.

•   That if you step on a grave in a cemetery, the deceased won't be comfortable until he has retaliated by coming around to haunt you some night.

•   That if you have a dream about falling, and actually "hit" before awakening, you will die.

Cities and States

- That as Maine goes so goes the nation.
- That New York, Washington, and Los Angeles are so far from the norm that people from those places cannot possibly know what the rest of the country is thinking.
- All New Yorkers are loud, New Englanders stoic, southerners slow, and Californians fast.
- That New Yorkers can live in a place for many years and never get to know their neighbors.
- That New York might be fun to visit, but no sensible person would live there.
- That civilization does not exist west of the Hudson River nor south of the Battery.
- That people in Los Angeles couldn't care less about either viewpoint—to them civilization is centered on the freeway.
- That people in New York City are offered so many cultural events that they find it hard to decide which to attend and therefore end up going to fewer plays, concerts, etcetera, than the average person from Milwaukee.
- That native Washingtonians are exceedingly hard to find in the

District of Columbia and that in the District you are much more likely to find someone born in Atlanta or Los Angeles.

• That there is no J Street in Washington, D.C.—between I and K Streets—because Pierre L'Enfant, who designed the city, was feuding with Chief Justice John Jay.

(An article by Jonathan Groner in *The Washington Post* stated, ". . . this story has not been proved false; but there appears to be no solid evidence supporting it and there probably never will be.")

• That children in Baltimore learn by their sixth birthday not to inhale through their noses because of: (a) the Exxon refinery in East Baltimore, (b) the mounds of rotting crab shells behind each house, and (c) the inner harbor. This odd way of breathing explains their accent.

• That residents of Pittsburgh have to remind themselves not to order boilermakers when they are out of town; that they are distinguished for calloused hands and incomprehensible accents.

• That Chicago is excessively windy and that anyone coming back from the "Windy City" should complain about how bad it was.

(Joseph Rosenbloom points out in his *Bananas Don't Grow on Trees* that Chicago, according to the U.S. Weather Bureau, ranks sixteenth on the list of the nation's windiest cities after such places as Boston and Dallas.)

• That to Iowans the smell of manure is the smell of money.

• That if tipped properly, any waitress in Nashville, Tennessee, will pick up her guitar and sing you a C & W song on the spot.

• That most of the people in New Orleans are decadents who carry on in the rich tradition of onetime resident Tennessee Williams, although some of the older folks are now slowing down and go to bed at four A.M. rather than dawn.

• That you still had best not speak evil of Huey Long in the rural backwoods of Louisiana, although you can risk a joke about Uncle Earl once the people get to know you.

That to Iowans the smell of manure is the smell of money.

- That a true Texan wears cowboy boots, a western hat, and chews Red Man.
- That the "real rich" oil men in Dallas, Houston, and Tulsa disdain Neiman-Marcus clothes and dress in the khakis and work boots they came to like while roughnecking in East Texas and the Permian Basin; their hobbies are collecting college football teams and Texas senators.

- That most of the people in Salt Lake City are Mormons, and federal law notwithstanding, polygamy persists, albeit oh, so quietly.
- That Las Vegas can be a cheap vacation if you don't gamble—they practically give the food away.
- That if you stand at the corner of Hollywood and Vine there is a good chance you will spot some of the top movie stars.
- That Los Angeles is without a downtown and therefore is "six suburbs in search of a city."
- That children in southern California are given a surfboard for their sixth birthday and admonished that they are now on their own.
- That the residents of Marin County, California, spend their weekends in hot tubs, sipping white wine and sighing.
- That the prettiest women in America are to be seen on the streets of Washington, Dallas, Houston, Los Angeles, Chicago, Philadelphia, Boston, or any one of 3,187 other cities and towns, depending on where the male watcher met his wife.
- That certain cities and towns are "Depression-proof" because of the basic nature of the goods or services that they provide (such as fuse boxes, oatmeal, and buttons).

(This claim is made by Chamber of Commerce people who forget that few, if any, places were spared by the economic ravages of the Great Depression.)

NEW YORK CREDOS OF 1930.

Writing in *Morrow's Almanack and Every-Day-Book for 1930* Burton Rascoe insisted that there was a "credo of the average New Yorker as distinct from the credo of residents of other cities." A small sampling from Rascoe's original set of thirty-nine:

- That Philadelphia is so dull and slow a town that the average citizen there doesn't know the Civil War is over.
- That the residents of Boston live exclusively on beans and codfish and that even streetcar conductors and coal heavers there use five-syllable words and talk like a page out of Emerson's essays.
- That Kalamazoo, Michigan, which is a great manufacturing city, must, because of its name, be a jerkwater town.
- That the patrons of New York nightclubs are exclusively out-of-town buyers who are painting the town red on company expense accounts.
- That mosquitoes grow as big as jaybirds in New Jersey.
- That all the residents of Brooklyn pronounce "early" as "oily" and "oily" as "early"; that they say "boids" for "birds" and "berl" for "boil."
- That there are deaths every week from falling elevators in department stores, but that the matter is hushed up by the newspapers for fear that the stores will withdraw their advertising.
- That before a girl can get a job in the chorus of a musical show she has to yield her virtue to the producer.
- That you can get a finer meal at the Automat than you can at the Ritz.
- That telephone operators at the switchboards of the big hotels invariably listen in on the conversation of the guests.

Crime

- That there is such a thing as "truth serum," but because of the Fifth Amendment it cannot be used to gain confessions from criminals.
- That holding one's breath for random intervals enables one to outsmart a lie detector machine; hardened criminals prefer a whiff of cocaine for insurance before their test.
- That the job of executioner is handed down from father to son, and that no one in the state save the prison warden knows his true identity.
- That a condemned man always orders an eccentric menu for his last meal, such as a pint of chocolate ice cream washed down with a six-pack of beer.
- That condemned criminals bellow for a minister and convert, the hour before they are put to death.
- That quicklime will destroy a corpse, and no self-respecting murderer should be without a supply of it.

(To quote from Philip Ward's *A Dictionary of Common Fallacies*, "Some writers of detective stories still labor under the odd delusion that quicklime will 'eat' a dead body, even though it helped to convict the multiple murderess Mrs. Belle Gunness of La Porte, Indiana, whose fourteen victims were excellently preserved in the telltale substance.")

• That the dons of organized crime are careful to ensure that outside "civilians" are never harmed in mob wars.

• That the reason the government has never *really* gone to work on the Mafia is because of the work the mob did for Uncle Sam during World War II.

• That every slice of pizza you eat puts seven cents into the hands of the Mafia, although no one is exactly sure of the routing of this money, and the economics of the particular sum cited.

• That the Mafia in the 1920s declared Washington, D.C., an "off-limits" city for organized crime to avoid attracting attention to itself; that the crime rate among members of Congress themselves makes the Mafia's nonpresence moot.

• That the Mafia has secret holds on certain members of Congress and the judiciary that enables it to subvert governmental processes.

• That there is no justice as satisfying as when a lenient judge is mugged or burglarized by the very kind of person he is always letting off easily.

• That fingerprints are commonly taken from the handles of revolvers and used to catch murderers.

(In real life this rarely happens. It is, however, common in fiction.)

• That mass murderers always impressed their neighbors and elementary school teachers as nice, quiet boys with good manners.

• That the most horrible crimes are committed by those on the lowest and uppermost levels of society.

• That the two easiest ways to acquire a vast sum of money in America are to engage in the smuggling of drugs or the bilking of the Medicaid system.

• That the police are never there when you need them, but always there when you go ten miles per hour over the limit.

• That a member of the Masonic order has never been hanged in the United States.

- That ground glass is an effective murder weapon.

(Unlike splintered glass, which is deadly, ground glass is virtually harmless. The authors of *The Prevalence of Nonsense* report that the seventeenth-century physician Sir Thomas Browne proved the point by giving a dog "above a dram thereof, subtilly powdered in Butter and Paste, without any visible disturbance.")

- That you cannot be accused of murder unless the body—the *corpus delicti*—is found.

(A number of murderers have been convicted after burning or otherwise disposing of their victims. Much of the confusion arises from the belief that the word *corpus* in *corpus delicti* refers to the corpse of the victim. The word actually refers to the body of the crime—i.e., proof that a crime has been committed.)

- That the eyes of the victim of a particularly vile murder will retain the image of the murderer.

- That the police always arrest or ticket the out-of-state driver first.

- That from time to time a counterfeiter comes along whose work is so good that the U.S. government does not prosecute for fear of shaking confidence in paper money.

- That one can be fined or imprisoned for killing a praying mantis.

- That it is illegal (and perhaps immoral) for a consumer to remove furniture tags—especially those attached to mattresses.

(The tag law originated as a health measure, to prevent the unrevealed resale of used mattresses and other stuffed material that might have been contaminated by earlier owners. Rest assured that you can remove a mattress tag without being hauled off to prison.)

- That from time to time a dishonest technician is able to instruct a computer to knock a few cents off all major financial transactions and has these pennies credited to his private account. The odd cents are never missed and within months the renegade computer technician has pocketed a million dollars and moved to Brazil.

(There have doubtlessly been a few cases like this, but the more sophisticated operators no longer satisfy themselves with pennies. In 1981 a Brazilian-born couple managed to siphon hundreds of thousands of dollars from a Washington, D.C., mutual fund and deposit the sum —by computer—in banks abroad. They were apprehended and convicted.)

Death

- That most deaths occur between the hours of two and six in the morning.
- That the recently deceased spent their next-to-last mortal week eating scores of dinners. This is evidenced by the number of people who say, "I can't believe he's dead. Just to think I had dinner with him last week."
- That certain Presidents are doomed to die in office because of the curse of the Twenty-Year Cycle.

(Supposedly, a President elected in a year divisible by twenty is destined to die in office. Through the 1980 election, nine men had been so elected; of these, six died during the immediate term—Harrison, 1840; Lincoln, 1860; Garfield, 1880; McKinley, 1900; Harding, 1920; and Kennedy, 1960. A seventh, Franklin Roosevelt, was also elected in a divisible-by-twenty year; he died during the term to which he was elected in 1944.)

- That when one confronts the possibility of sudden death one's life flashes in front of one's eyes.
- That there are a number of documented cases in which a clock has stopped working when its owner died.

- That you drown when you go down for the third time.
- That at the moment of death there is an immediate loss of a tiny amount of weight.

Drink

- That the best beer is brewed from mountain stream water.
- That the Japanese can drink infinitely more sake, Russians and Poles more vodka, Mexicans more tequila, than you can—and still stay sober.

- That people are often frozen, bitten by poisonous snakes, or thrown from cars, but survive because they are totally inebriated.
- That you can drink more highballs than cocktails even if the amount of liquor in each is equal.
- That champagne produces the worst of all hangovers.
- That cheap jug wine will usually beat expensive imported wine in blind tastings. Ditto for plain club soda, which will top imported sparkling water.
- That vodka has no taste. That all vodka is the same, so you may as well go out and buy a cheap one.
- That moving men have learned how to get drunk during a day's work without anyone ever seeing the bottle.
- That a single jigger of absinthe will either kill you or render you blind. That a single jigger of olive oil, consumed pre-festivities, will keep you sober and upright for the evening. That twelve jiggers of beer, consumed in rapid succession, will render immobile even the most renowned of collegiate drinkers.
- That various American millionaire families such as the Fricks, the Mellons, and the Fords are still drinking up the wine stocks their forefathers laid in just before Prohibition.
- That those ten-thousand-dollar bottles of wine sold at fancy auctions turn to vinegar once uncorked.
- That the Allied advance across Europe in the Second World War was delayed for weeks because troops stopped to "liberate" wine cellars.
- That actor Paul Newman is the only man in America who can drink twenty-four cans of beer daily and keep that kind of waistline.
- That from time to time an old wino is spotted with a tarnished Phi Beta Kappa key hanging from his ravaged body.

(This is often embellished with the testimony of someone who actually saw such a key. In one version, a family is driving in New York City and gets lost in the Bowery. An old derelict looms into view as the car stops for a red light. He cleans the windshield with a dirty old rag in hopes of getting a few coins from the driver. As he leans over to wipe the other side of the windshield, the key is pressed against the glass.)

• That it is somehow worse to see a completely drunken woman than a totally soused man.

• That the mixture of aspirin and Coca-Cola is (a) a powerful intoxicant, (b) a powerful aphrodisiac, but, either way, (c) can kill you.

• That if you put a tooth in a glass of Coca-Cola overnight, it will have dissolved by morning. This is also true of a nail or a penny.

(Many experimenters have proven this false, including our friend Bob Skole, who had a tooth extracted in March 1982 that is presumably still sitting in a bottle of Coke in his bathroom.)

(There are so many stories about Coca-Cola in circulation that the neologism "Cokelore" is used in folklore journals to refer to the phenomenon. These range from a host of fables having to do with foreign objects found in Coke bottles [in many of these the finder is offered vast sums in out-of-court settlements] to fanciful stories about the ends to which the company goes to protect its secret formula. In his *Dictionary of Misinformation* Tom Burnam tells of the popular myth in which the company is allowed to leap suddenly from a small operation to a multi-million-dollar international corporation. According to this story, back in the days when Coke was sold only at soda fountains, a man came to the officers of the company and told them that for five hundred dollars he would reveal the secret of untold corporate riches. He was given the five hundred dollars and announced the secret: "Bottle it!")

• That the Mafia introduced 7-Up during Prohibition to encourage young women to drink whiskey.

Education

- That teachers in private schools took only academic courses in college and thus were not contaminated by pedagogical courses; the reverse is true for teachers in public schools.
- That if you had been given the money to fund four years in college when you were eighteen, and invested it in the stock market, you wouldn't have to work for a living now.

(Such computations can be made to work only when they allow that you were smart enough to buy IBM and Xerox at two bits a share.)

- That there is no idea which is so farfetched that it is not believed and advocated by at least six professors and a handful of California psychologists.
- That people with MBAs from Harvard Business School have immense power over the day-to-day conduct of American life.

(To be sure, MBAs have power, but nothing like the amount ascribed to them by some.)

- That children learn much faster than adults and that it is futility personified for a person to try to learn anything *really* new after his fortieth birthday.

• That memorizing something complex will improve your "memory power."

• That for all the aptitude testing done by companies, the armed forces, and educational institutions, no relationship has been demonstrated between later success and test scores (Stanines, GREs, LSATs, DATs, MCATs, College Boards, etcetera).

• That the study of mathematics develops a more logical mind.

• That no man is truly educated until he has read the Bible.

(A once reasonable thought, but one that has been stated solemnly so many times that it has become the crustiest of clichés.)

• That the better educated are necessarily of better character.

• That studying Latin will improve your vocabulary.

• Those who can, do. Those who can't, teach. Those who can't teach, teach teachers.

Famous People

- That if Hank Aaron had played for a New York or Los Angeles team he would have been lionized earlier, more intensely, and longer.
- That Warren Beatty is just as much a huntsman of female flesh as the gossip magazines claim him to be.
- That if it had not been for Elizabeth Taylor, Richard Burton would have been the greatest actor in the English-speaking world.
- That Betty Crocker and Sara Lee were not only real people but first-class cooks.
- That Walter Cronkite would make an infinitely better President, senator, or astronaut than anyone he has ever interviewed on television.
- That Thomas Dewey would have been elected President if he had not looked like a paper doll.
- That John Dillinger had an enormous member which has been preserved and is now kept under lock and key in a dusty corner of the Smithsonian.

(Another version of this, preferred by those who "know" Washington, is that Dillinger's privates are to be found in formaldehyde in a jar at the Armed Forces Medical Museum, which is on the grounds of the

Walter Reed Army Medical Center on Sixteenth Street. An intrepid reporter from the monthly *Washington Tribune* actually went out to check on this story. It was not on public view, and he was too embarrassed to ask the curator if it was there. "Hell, I don't get paid enough to go out on a limb like that," wrote the reporter, Michael Leccese, in a moment of deep journalistic candor.)

• That the man who is languishing in Spandau Prison in West Germany is not really Rudolf Hess. Hess escaped Germany in 1945, flew to Paraguay in a borrowed glider, and his place in prison was taken by his perfect double, Klaus von Spangenberg. Hess operates a flying school in Asunción, Paraguay.

• That Adolf Hitler was a paperhanger.

(Nor was he a housepainter, as is sometimes alleged. He was an artist, actually.)

• That Herbert Hoover was probably a better President than granted by historians, but he didn't know how to handle the media.

• That within hours of J. Edgar Hoover's death, President Nixon had troops seize the FBI director's infamous "personal files" and transport them to San Clemente. In due course Nixon intends to use this material to blackmail his way back into politics.

• That Howard Hughes really fooled us all, and that in ten years or so he will reappear and regain his empire; he was flash-frozen by an unknown California scientist and is being stored in a vault in the West in a state of suspended animation.

• That David Janssen was the illegitimate son of Clark Gable.

• That Elton John and Olivia Newton-John were once married.

• That the small set of initials, JS, immediately below FDR's head on the Roosevelt dime stand for Josef Stalin and appear there through some sinister political plot.

(This belief grew in the months following the debut of the new dime in early 1946. The JS stands for artist John Sinnock. The Treasury

Department was finally required to issue an official denial of the Stalin charge.)

• That the marking at the base of John F. Kennedy's neck on the fifty-cent piece is a hammer and sickle—perhaps put there by the same invisible hand that put JS on the dime.

• That JFK had been married once before he married Jackie.

(Although the tale is not nearly as prevalent as it was before the 1960 election, there are still people who believe that this was one of the major cover-ups of the twentieth century.)

• That Nikita Khrushchev was a playful bear and that the highlight of his life was his visit to Disneyland.

• That although General Douglas MacArthur was sort of a nut, his accomplishments nonetheless made him a valuable soldier.

(MacArthur was renowned for a preening ego that prompted him to demand personal credit for all triumphs in his command, regardless of his role. MacArthur tolerated neither dissent nor criticism.)

• That MacArthur delayed his arrival in the Philippines until he was assured that newsreel cameras were present to record his "I Shall Return" march through the surf; no Japanese soldier was within miles.

• That while playing for the Dallas Cowboys, Don Meredith was secretly married to both Tom Landry's daughter and ex-Cleveland Browns football coach Blanton Collier's daughter.

• That Sir Isaac Newton was beaned by an apple, which led him to wrap up his laws of gravity.

• That Richard Nixon was able to open relations with Red China because of, not despite, his Republican, anticommunist background. If Hubert Humphrey or George McGovern had tried it, the American people would not have stood for such a "sellout."

• That FDR sold us down the river at Yalta.

• That one of the judges that Roosevelt tried to pack the Supreme Court with didn't have a law degree.

(Such an appointment would have done no harm to the U.S. Constitution or federal law; neither requires that a federal judge at any level be an attorney.)

• That Willie Sutton robbed banks "because that was where the money was."

("I never said it," Sutton stated in his memoir. "The credit belongs to some enterprising reporter who apparently felt a need to fill out his copy." But Sutton liked the phrase so much, he entitled his memoir *Where the Money Was*.)

• That a major reason why Robert A. Taft failed in three attempts to get the Republican presidential nomination was his unfortunate set of initials (which would have provided a succession from FDR to HST to RAT).

• That George Washington had wooden teeth.
(His teeth were actually made of ivory.)

• That great historical figures required very little sleep.

• That a number of prominent Americans have been secret members of the Ku Klux Klan.

• That most great men and women were born of poor but honest parents.

THREE W. C. FIELDS MYTHS

• That Uncle Claude's tombstone contains the inscription "All things considered, I'd rather be in Philadelphia." Actually, Fields has no tombstone. He was cremated—at his behest—on June 3, 1949, some thirty months after his death; his ashes repose in niche 20805 of the Columbarium of Nativity, The Great Mausoleum, Forest Lawn Memorial Park, Glendale, California. The oft-repeated quotation was given by Fields to a writer for *Vanity Fair*

Magazine in 1937 who asked movie stars what inscription they would choose for their gravestones.

• That Uncle Claude, in a self-description, said, "No man who hates dogs and children can be all bad." Comedians take material where it can be found. In this instance, the remark apparently was uttered by Byron Darnton of *The New York Times*, after listening to a bore at a cocktail party. The *bon mot* got into print in *Harper's* magazine in 1930, attributed to Darnton.

• That Uncle Claude so distrusted the world of finance that he opened bank accounts in numerous institutions under assumed names, often in the company of his boon companion John Barleycorn, and was unable to remember them later. Consequently, he lost scores of thousands of dollars. To the contrary, according to testimony at a hearing on the probate of his will, Fields was a painstaking records-keeper, for he listed no less than twenty-three separate bank accounts he opened between 1903 and 1946, the year he died.

(Will Fowler, the California writer who discovered martinis at Fields's knee at age thirteen, in the company of father Gene Fowler, gently dispels these Fields stories in his *The Second Handshake*, Lyle Stuart, Inc., Secaucus, N. J., 1980. Fowler avows that the "tombstone" legend is regularly repeated on TV talk shows by "Fields experts" whose portfolios consist of "a sheet of the comedian's personal stationery with a letter addressed to another person.")

Fashion

- That women's—and, increasingly, men's—fashions are controlled by a small clique with foreign accents. This clique has a mysterious lock on every department-store buyer in America.
- That clothes are designed by men who hate women.
- That hunters should wear red for safety.

(The National Safety Council says that fluorescent orange is better, especially at dawn and dusk when red is hard to see.)

- That only older men wear boxer shorts.
- That rats are systematically bred in South African sewers, made into fur coats, and exported to the United States disguised as mink, ermine, and seal.

(This story was picked up by the Associated Press from the Johannesburg *Star* and appeared in a number of American newspapers before it was discovered to be a 1980 April Fool joke. Retractions notwithstanding, the story continues to make the rounds as fact verified by the AP. One editor wrote of his paper, "The cynical, sharp-eyed, suspicious wire-desk editors at the St. Petersburg *Times* bought the story hook, line, and sinker.")

- That red flannel is warmer than white.
- That ashes are good for carpets, especially cigar ashes.
- That the color of pea soup is good for the eyes and spirit, which is why the bulkheads of Navy ships, the innards of the Pentagon, and most of the walls in civilian government agencies are painted in this bilious green.

Fill in

the Blanks

A collection of credos that take on different nouns at different times and places.

- That ——————— is not really dead, but survives in a coma in a heavily guarded hospital room in ———————.
  (Perhaps the commonest version has John F. Kennedy in a coma at Parkland Hospital, where Jacqueline Onassis still secretly visits him once a month, but it is also applied to other popular figures ranging from James Dean to John Lennon.)

- That money donated to ——————— is covertly channeled into paying for ———————.
  (One version of this, which circulated a few years ago, had the March of Dimes supporting the abortion of fetuses suspected of having birth defects.)

- That free speech is a fine thing but that it has been taken too

far in the case of —————————, who should be brought under control.
   •   That because an engineer once misplaced a decimal point, a large, brand-new ————————— collapsed.
   •   That the major oil companies are repressing the technology that would allow the conversion of plentiful, inexpensive ————————— into a source of energy.
   •   That the world is divided into two classes of people; those who ————————— and those who don't.
   •   That if all the money that has been spent by Americans on ————————— had been applied to the problem of —————————, the problem would be solved by now.
   •   That we can put men on the moon, yet we can't even —————————.

   •   That a group of hoodlums called the ————————— Rats terrorized the streets of ————————— during the forties and fifties/fifties and sixties/sixties and seventies.
   (If all the stories of the Rats were true, they would have overpowered the U.S. Armed Forces at peak strength. A common epilogue tacked onto the Rats story is that the members are grown up, have children of their own, and are respected members of the community.)
   •   That the ————————— house at ————————— College/University was the model for the movie *Animal House.*
   •   That ————————— was the model for *Dr. Strangelove.*
   (There are many Strangeloves, but the most commonly cited are Herman Kahn, Henry Kissinger, and Wernher von Braun.)
   •   That if you collect enough —————————, they can be exchanged for a kidney dialysis machine.
   (This is a cruel credo that causes the National Kidney Foundation to be occasionally given mountains of cigarette wrappers, box tops, tea bag envelopes, or whatever.)

- That if you give a ———————— one drink of hard liquor, he'll drink the whole bottle.

(Said of Germans by Swedes, Danes by Germans, etcetera)

- That the main ingredient of ———————— is sugar.
- That the Red Cross charges the going rate or more for ———————— during major disasters and World Wars.

(The blank in this amazingly virulent untruism can be filled with coffee, doughnuts, sandwiches, or blood. Red Cross villainy of this sort was a part of the folklore of World War II—along with the completely unfounded belief that the Red Cross was charging GIs in Iceland high prices for sweaters that were knitted by American volunteers—and hangs on to this day. In 1961 the *DAV Magazine,* published by the Disabled American Veterans, carried an editorial attacking the doughnut myth, which said in part, "Like so many such stories this one has faded from reality to legend. It's sort of like having been chewed out by Patton . . . or having to eat spoiled field rations . . . or drinking hair tonic strained through bread. We all did it. You just aren't anyone who was anyone if you didn't have to pay for your Red Cross donuts during World War II."

(A few years ago one of the coauthors of this book was interviewing Red Cross President George M. Elsey, and the subject of the organization's never-ending campaign to spike the coffee, sandwich, and doughnut rumor came up. "Not long ago," he said, "I appeared on a television show in Hawaii on which viewers were allowed to call in and ask me questions. An irate man called in to charge that we had sold sandwiches when Agnes brought heavy flooding to Elmira, New York, which, as always, was not true.")

- That some time ago a ———————— with an experimental engine was accidentally sold to an unsuspecting consumer who was bowled over when he found it got 125 miles to the gallon. The mistake was discovered, and the man was paid a vast sum for the car and his silence.

(What is never made clear about this story is why Mazda, VW, Ford, or whoever is holding this development back when it could, in fact, give the company an overwhelming sales advantage. Could it be the dark hand of the oil companies?)

Food

- That Howard Johnson's once had good food.
- That it's just as well that we do not know the true contents of hot dogs sold by sidewalk vendors.
- That if you befriend the maître d' of a small French restaurant and exchange a few words in French with him each time you enter, the chef will ensure that you are served the best chop from the kitchen, and a bottle of wine "reserved for our best customers" will be offered to you. But be prepared to pay a tip of at least twenty-five percent if you want a table the next time you visit, and don't examine the label on the wine bottle too closely.
- That a roadside restaurant with many trucks parked outside is ipso facto a good place to eat.
- That a good way to determine whether or not a Chinese restaurant is any good is to see if many Orientals are eating there. If there are only non-Orientals dining, chances are that the food is not very good.
- That in order for a deli to be any good: (1) the waiters must be thoroughly obnoxious, and (2) at least one very fat man with a pinky ring must be seated and eating near the front door.
- That restaurants make all their money on booze and lose or break even on food no matter how it is priced.

college, I was traveling through the backwaters of Mexico, searching for experience [as students are wont to do]. Eschewing the beaten path, I found myself one evening drinking in a Mexican workers' bar in an unnamed small town near the Arizona border. After my third or fourth strong—but awful-tasting—taste of tequila, I happened to inquire of one of the drinking workers where I could purchase some of the *good* tequila I'd heard so much about. [The stuff they drink there is real p***-water.] Turning to me he replied, in broken English, 'Good tequila? Yes, I had good tequila once . . . in Wisconsin!' " Summation: The Mexican credo in play here appears to be a corollary to the American credo that one can't get a good steak in Kansas City—to wit, that all good tequila is shipped to the wealthier United States market.)

• That a person has to be born in Mississippi to eat possum stew and keep it down.

• That it is wrong and unhealthful to consume either milk and pickles or milk and shellfish at the same sitting.

• That the most outwardly rigid devotees of natural foods occasionally sneak a Twinkie, Devil Dog, or fistful of Pringle's.

• That cornbread should never be cut with a knife, but should be broken.

• That antifreeze is a common ice-cream ingredient.

• That chocolate is addictive, causes pimples, and in certain cases acts as an aphrodisiac.

• That certain types of junk foods are impregnated with secret chemicals that act as "appetite aphrodisiacs," making the eater unable to stop after a sensible amount of munching.

• That red M&M's have aphrodisiacal qualities, which is why they are so hard to find.

• That brown eggs are more nutritious than white ones. Also, eggs that are consumed on a farm are vastly superior to those bought in a store.

That red M&M's have aphrodisiacal qualities, which is why they are so hard to find.

(The ageless line that the visitor must utter when having farm eggs: "You know, it's impossible to get eggs like this in the city.")

• That the smell of a pink or green chemical mouthwash is less offensive than that of garlic.

• That banquet food is by definition bad and comprised of rubber chicken, pebblelike peas, and wilted salad.

• That if a drinking glass is ever used to hold gasoline, the taste will remain no matter how many times the vessel is washed.

• That cane sugar is sweeter than beet sugar.

• That tea is more healthful than coffee.

• That eating green apples will cause a terrible stomachache.

• That fish is brain food.

• That the addition of cottage cheese and a pear-half to a meal reduces its caloric total.

• That when you are told there will be a twenty-minute wait for a table, and would-you-like-to-wait-in-the-bar, you can expect to have time for three drinks before your name is called.

Government

- That the federal bureaucracy has purposely interpreted and enforced laws so as to undermine confidence in those laws.

(Popular mythology has it that devious bureaucrats have, for instance, discredited endangered species acts by chasing elderly women in ancient fur coats rather than going after poachers and importers.)

- That our government is there to protect us.
- That government assistance programs usually do more harm than good.
- That nothing is so simple that it can be accomplished efficiently by the government.
- That you cannot solve a problem by throwing money at it.
- That the statue atop the U.S. Capitol is that of a pregnant Indian woman and symbolizes the birth of the nation.

(It was revealed in *The Washington Post* of October 3, 1977, that this myth was intentionally spread by Bob Sanders, a Capitol policeman, who told it to vast numbers of tourists.)

- That the government sells jeeps at auction every month in Arizona (or perhaps North Carolina) for two hundred dollars each, but friends and relatives of master sergeants have the market cornered.

•   That people routinely overlooked by the nation's massive welfare system are the saddest and most needy, but that there is always room on the rolls for a glib loafer.

•   That there are bureaucrats in the federal government who have spent years in unmarked offices, doing not a lick of work during the day, their existence unknown even to their nominal superiors. They write novels, listen to the radio, and take four-hour lunch breaks while we taxpayers give them thirty-five thousand dollars a year.

•   That key government officials know more about the Russians, the Mafia, and the Kennedys than the rest of us can ever hope to learn.

•   That no matter how democratic a nation, its diplomats will always be highborn.

•   That if the Postal Service were entirely turned over to private enterprise it would become much more efficient.

•   That a letter without a zip code will travel as quickly as or more quickly than one without. We put them on letters because we are told to do so.

•   That you should be aware that the coded numbers that appear on the peel-off label on your federal tax form can trigger an audit.

•   That there was never any gold at Fort Knox.

•   That from time to time there is a case in which a child will murder his parents and then get government survivor benefits as an orphan.

(Remarkably, until a short time ago this was true. The Social Security Administration found that it had paid in two such cases in California. The loophole has presumably been closed, as Social Security officials have advised field offices not to process claims from "survivors who may have been involved in an intentional act which resulted in the death of a parent.")

•   That the FBI has a master switchboard on Eighth Street SE or on New York Avenue that permits agents to listen to any conversation on any telephone line in the world. Transcripts are computerized and fed into citizens' dossiers. Former Attorney General Ramsey Clark did not fire J. Edgar Hoover, because the FBI director knew, from his files, how many bottles of Shiner Beer Clark drank at a University of Texas fraternity house party in the 1940s.

•   That if you build a house and don't put on front steps, it will be considered "unfinished," and you will not have to pay real estate taxes.

Health
and Medicine

- That new miracle drugs of potentially great—perhaps revolutionary—benefit to humanity are being kept off the market by bureaucrats and regulators in Washington who are subjecting them to years of unneeded testing and bogging them down in tons of paperwork.
- That vast numbers of Americans die, within weeks, of physical examinations at which they were deemed to be in good health.
- That M.D.s know next to nothing about either nutrition or sex.
- That medical doctors must know Latin.
- That the comeuppance of modern medicine is that it has done nothing to cure the common cold.
- That all doctors have atrocious handwriting, which is a function of their frenzied note-taking in medical school.
- That all medical doctors play golf.

(No less august an organization than the American Medical Association conducted a survey in 1979 to prove that a mere eleven percent of the nation's doctors play the game.)

- That medical doctors are taught to write prescriptions in a secret code that only they and the druggist can understand.

- That sponges used in surgery are frequently forgotten and left inside the patient. Each operating room has an attendant whose duty it is to record the passing of sponges, but he or she is frequently distracted. These omissions cause no problems for the negligent doctor, for at the insistence of the insurance companies, a variety of sponge has been developed that cannot be detected by X rays. Hence malpractice suits are impossible.
- That brushing one's teeth with plain baking soda, or even salt, is a more effective antidote to tooth decay than those high-priced pastes.
- That there are no brave men in a dentist's office.
- That you should never open windows at night, as the night air causes disease.
- That excesses in lechery, rich food, and strong drink are the chief causes of gout, which most often afflicts men of exceptional talent and bank accounts.
- That sex will clear up acne.
- That wearing garlic around the neck protects the wearer from whatever epidemic is making the rounds.
- That drinking cold water on a hot day can kill you, that running with a stick in your hand will "poke your eye out," that reading in a badly lit room will cause you to go blind.
- That going outside after washing your hair will cause pneumonia and possibly lead to your demise.
- That you should feed a cold and starve a fever.

(From an article on popular misconception in *Family Safety* magazine: "This old saw [it goes back in some form or other to Roman times] has been repeatedly attacked but still crops up. One doctor who fought it asked that the phrase 'He fed fevers' be inscribed on his tombstone.")

- That if you get frostbite, you should rub the injured area with snow.

(Today's favored remedy, according to the National Safety Council, is warm water, but never hot water.)

- That Americans have the best health care in the world.
- That if you cross your eyes and the wind changes, they will stay that way.
- That wearing a hat inside the house will cause you to get a headache.
- That a summer cold is more tenacious than a winter cold and will therefore hang on longer.
- That regularity—that is, a bowel movement at roughly the same time each day—is the right and healthy human condition.
- That the skin breathes and that certain cosmetics aid that breathing.
- That sleeping outside increases your resistance to colds and other illnesses.
- That an enormous appetite is a symptom of having a tapeworm.
- That every time you hiccup it means that you are growing.
- That freezing kills germs.
- That sleepwalkers are generally immune to harm.
- That if a grown man gets mumps, he will become sterile.

(John Camp reports in his *Magic, Myth and Medicine* that a London hospital team studied two hundred men who had mumps and could find no evidence of an inability to father.)

- That swallowing seeds (watermelon seeds, for example) will cause appendicitis.
- That you should put nothing in your ear smaller than your elbow.
- That sea air is particularly good for your health.
- That it is possible to build up one's resistance to the common cold.

That you should put nothing in your ear smaller than your elbow.

• That unless you have a lamp on in the room, watching television will ruin the children's eyes, as well as your own.

(This myth was created in the early 1950s by an innovative Philadelphia public relations man named J. Robert Mendte, on behalf of a client who manufactured lamps.)

Historic

- That when you visit the bedroom of an historic home you can show how observant you are by commenting that people used to be much shorter.

(The preliminary results of a seven-university study of such things indicates that early Americans were not significantly shorter than they are today. The average man in the time of the Revolutionary War was only an inch shorter than today's average.)

- That we are living in a relatively dull period that lacks the vigor and innovation of other times.

(This credo has apparently been common to many periods. In Stephen Fovargue's *A New Catalogue of Vulgar Errors* published in 1767 we are told that a common fallacy of the time was the belief that that period was duller and less ingenious than those past.)

- That all the great American fortunes were amassed originally by robber barons, economic buccaneers, or wandering old drunks who happened to get lucky at the right time.

- That under the terms of its original admission to the Union, Texas can divide into five separate states, and that if the federal govern-

- That frightful experiences or grief will cause one
white overnight.

- That you can cure hiccups by drinking a glass o
as you can without stopping. Or by eating a tablespoon c
having someone jump out at you behind a closet door, s;
Or by holding your breath for as long as you can.

- That it is dangerous to swim for an hour after
Eating causes debilitating stomach cramps.

(Physicians scoff at this belief; its chief utility seems
giving parents a brief respite after lunch before returnin;
with energetic children.)

- That wearing rubber overshoes inside the house
host of unspecified illnesses.

- That "cellulite" is different from, and therefore r
than, plain old ordinary fat.

- That if you take a large enough dose of poison,
you. Similarly, if you take a tiny, tiny dose of poison ever
gradually build up an immunity to that poison.

- That anyone who has lived to be over one hun
whiskey, tobacco, or both, for most of his life.

ment ever becomes outrageously ornery, ten Texas senators will be in Washington rather than two.

- That history is destined to repeat itself.
- That just west of the Azores in ten thousand feet of water lies the hulk of the German freighter *Deutschland.* It was scuttled there in 1945 with its cargo of $150 million in gold bullion, following the collapse of the Third Reich. This fortune will be used to fund the rise of the Fourth Reich. This could happen any day now.

TIME CAPSULE—1950s COLD WAR INTERLUDE

- That if our army had kept driving across Europe and conquered Russia, we wouldn't have all these postwar problems; that namby-pamby diplomats prevented the military from achieving total victory.
- That although some of Joe McCarthy's tactics were pretty rough, he did a good job in running Commies out of government.
- That if we had threatened to use the A-bomb on Joe Stalin if he didn't behave, he would have become a decent world citizen instantly.
- That the Truman administration "lost China" through the same bungling that prevented total victory in the war.

- That quadruple amputees were sent home during World War II without giving their families warning of their condition. Commonly a man's wife or mother would arrive at the town railroad station to find her "wounded" GI in a basket.

(This belief, which lives on to this day, was extremely common during

the war and the decade following. Actually, there were only two in-
dividuals who lost all four limbs during the war. Both these men were
greeted as heroes by both the government and the public, which lavished
gifts upon them.)

• That history texts used south of the Mason-Dixon line never say
Civil War, but rather the War between the States.

• That the Hope diamond and the mummy of King Tut have
eternal curses attached to them.

• That the stock market crash and ensuing Depression caused the
suicide rate to rise alarmingly. That great numbers of able-bodied men
spent the period selling apples on street corners.

(There were, of course, suicides and apple sellers, but nothing approx-
imating what has been built up in the popular imagination. Apple sellers
were a convenient subject for photographers who needed a human picture of what was initially an economic event.)

• That Mussolini made the trains run on time.

(In their book *The Prevalence of Nonsense* Ashley Montagu and
Edward Darling said of this credo, "There was little or no truth in it;
people who lived in Italy between the March on Rome (October 28,
1922) and the execution at Como (1945) will bear testimony to the fact
that Italian railroads remained as insouciant as ever with regard to
timetables and actual schedules. It made no difference to the myth; it
never makes any difference. . . .")

• That a number of American doughboys and GIs returned home
after two world wars because the bullets that hit them were deflected
by Bibles or prayer books that they carried in their breast pockets.

• That up to and well into the 1970s aging Japanese soldiers would
regularly emerge from the jungles of the South Pacific to finally surren-
der. In all probability there are still a few of these World War II
stragglers at large.

(Yellowed newsclippings prove that there were some stragglers who held on for quite a while after the war was over, but popular mythology turned a few holdouts into legions.)

•   That nobody still knows what really caused the Civil War or the Depression.

•   That no matter what year it happens to be, it is the general consensus that fifteen years earlier: (1) great antiques were cheap and plentiful, (2) food tasted better, (3) there were more fish, (4) things were not as complicated, and (5) people were generally happier.

That they don't make 'em like they used to.

- That they don't make 'em, like they used to (cars, ice cream cones, ball players, politicians, soldiers, bicycles, pocket combs, typewriters, philosophers, portable radios, grandmothers, books, hamburgers, manservants, family doctors, and a lot of other stuff).
- That television shows were better twenty years ago, and that the radio shows twenty years before were even better.
- That during the period during which American hostages were held in Iran, Iranian students in the United States were able to stay out of harm's way by wearing yarmulkes.
- That Sweeney Todd ("the demon barber of Fleet Street") was a real person who once sold meat pies made of human flesh.

WORLD WAR II INTERLUDE

- That the Japanese had poor vision due to their slanted eyes and would be worthless as fighter pilots.
- That most Japanese armament was made from American scrap metal, and the familiar logos of U.S. auto companies could occasionally be found on artillery shells.
- That if the American people ever learned the real truth about Pearl Harbor, President Roosevelt would have been impeached.

(New evidence published by historian John Toland in his 1982 book *Infamy!* suggests [but does not emphatically prove] that the suspicions were well founded: that FDR in fact did know of the Japanese plans in advance of the attack.)

- That the average German officer wore a monocle, a gray greatcoat, and rode around the battlefield in an open touring car, clicking his heels smartly at the sight of a superior.
- That German submarines regularly sank convoys of Ameri-

can ships only a few miles off the U.S. coast, and residents could see them burning on the horizon; censorship prevented this news from appearing in print.

• That the Pentagon was staffed exclusively by armchair commandos who had priority for Scotch whiskey rations, gave silk stockings to their blond girl friends, and relied on old college classmates to keep them out of battle.

• That large numbers of Vietnam vets are walking time bombs who will explode when given the right stimulus.

(All wars produce psychological victims and Vietnam was no exception, but somewhere along the line this insidious preconception took hold. Television melodramas featuring exploding Vietnam vets have fed the myth.)

The Human
Condition

- That humans are the only species capable of cannibalism.
- That the human race is the only species that is sexually active all year long.
- That the human race is the only species that kills its own kind. (This credo is usually hauled out in wartime to underscore the horrors of human nature. There are many examples, including the female praying mantis, which, as a matter of course, kills and devours its mate during or just after mating.)
- That an intense stare at the back of another can make that other person turn around.
- That there is no human custom—no matter how disgusting, unnatural, or immoral—that anthropologists have not found to be the norm among the members of remote tribes.
- That the "average man" drives a cab, which therefore means that particular notice should be made of the opinions of cabbies.
- That there are two sides to every question.
- That the heart is the seat of the mind.

- That you get what you pay for.
- That all major disasters come in threes.
- That next year's model will be better.
- That popular notions can be believed because they represent the accumulated wisdom of the people and that if they were totally or substantially incorrect we would have stopped repeating them long ago.

(This may be regarded as the keystone credo and may, in fact, be the most wrongheaded of them all. Few have so successfully stated the case as Albert E. Wiggam in his myth-baiting classic *The Marks of a Clear Mind:* "Popular notions are always wrong," he wrote, adding, "The so-called 'accumulated wisdom of the ages' . . . is mostly accumulated tommy-rot.")

- That it is the exception which proves the rule.

(Logic dictates that the exception disproves the rule.)

- That it is virtually impossible for a person to change.
- That practice makes perfect.

(Practice can make perfect, but it often has the effect of compounding error, driving out spontaneity, or simply making things slightly better. A bad actor or high jumper cannot practice his way to perfection.)

- That one must pay one's dues, whatever that means.
- That nothing is ever as much fun as you remember it being.
- That time flies when you're having fun.
- That it is not what you know but who you know.
- That good will eventually win out.
- That what you see is what you get.
- That a rising tide lifts all boats.
- That money can't buy happiness.
- That beginners are blessed with good luck.
- That to be a genius is to lack common sense.
- That there are certain questions that can never be satisfactorily answered; for example, "What came first, the chicken or the egg?" or

"If a tree falls in the forest when no person or animal is near, does it actually make a noise?"

• That the crossing of letters in the mail is evidence of something more than mere coincidence.

• That no one sleeps well the first time he lies down in a new bed.

• That even though the United Nations is ineffective, it is the best hope we have.

That money can't buy happiness.

"I" Witnesses

Some clichéd thought takes the form of individual declarations that are heard so often that they sound as though they are sung by a chorus— "I hate cats but I love kittens," for instance, or "I can still get [*exaggerated number*] miles to the gallon in my old car." Technically, these declarations are not credos, but they are from the same family.

- That I was thinking about you just before you called. (Variation: That I was thinking about you just before your letter arrived.)
- That I can get to my office in a flat twenty minutes.
- That I never watch television except for documentaries and sports.
- That I am not superstitious but I don't take unreasonable chances, either, so I don't walk under ladders, will not accept two-dollar bills, avoid the thirteenth floor of buildings (especially on Friday the thirteenth), and never, never count the number of cars in a funeral procession.
- That it isn't the money, it's the principle of the thing.
- That I don't know much about art, but I do know what I like.

That if it weren't for the children, we'd live in the city.

•   That large numbers of checks are in the mail.

(This, of course, comes from the oft-heard declaration that the check is in the mail. Another credo to go with it, "That millions of postcards are lost annually." When people come back from vacation, they often say, "Didn't you get the postcard I sent you? It's amazing how bad the mail has gotten.")

•   That if it weren't for the children we'd live in the city.

•   That there is something intrinsically wrong with public opinion polls because neither I nor anybody I know has ever been contacted for one.

•   That I have a sense of humor.

(No American, no matter how sullen, will admit to not having a sense of humor.)

•   That I usually break even when I go to Las Vegas.

•   I know it looks like I've been overeating. The truth is that it is my metabolism—that is, my body retains a lot of water. And I haven't ruled out the possibility that it's glandular.

•   That flea markets are generally dreadful affairs, but I have made some stunning finds at them.

(If all the tales of great flea market finds were true, there would be no need for a Social Security system, since we would all have a closet full of Paul Revere silver, Stradivarius violins, and the like to sell during our old age.)

•   That Polish jokes are rude and demeaning to a proud nationality, but while I'm thinking about it, have you heard about the Pole who . . .

Journalism

- That if at some odd hour of the night you are determined to know the name of the last left-handed National League pitcher to hit a triple with two on in the World Series, you can call the city desk of any large newspaper and someone will know the answer.
- That writing for a newspaper so dulls one's talent that no readable literature has ever been produced by a former journalist.
- That writing for a newspaper teaches one the discipline necessary to produce readable literature.
- That writing for a newspaper is irrelevant to one's literary future.
- That journalists are irresponsible whelps who do not have to suffer the consequences of their actions; nonetheless, freedom of the press must be preserved lest the Republic collapse.
- That newspaper columnists are able to spit out 750 words of compelling prose in twenty minutes flat with all sorts of noise and commotion going on around them.
- That you should never buy the newspaper on the top of the pile.
- That newspapers are written at a sixth-grade reading level.
- That blown-dry anchormen on local television news shows get to know the "pulse of the people" by appearing at shopping-center

promotional events, an activity far more valuable, journalistically, than actually reporting a story from time to time.

- That there is no real difference between *Time* and *Newsweek*.
- That the New York–Washington-based liberal media haven't the foggiest notion of what is going on in the rest of the country.
- That the *National Enquirer* is now respectable because it no longer runs articles about parents who made soup of infants. Buying a copy at the A & P is permissible because we need to know what "they" are reading. To ignore this periodical would be snobbism of the worst degree.
- That newspapermen are hard-bitten, cynical, and know far more than they dare put into print.
- That if you wish to monitor the thinking of the average American all you have to do is to listen to Paul Harvey.
- That in order for something to appear in the *Reader's Digest*, it must have appeared somewhere else before; in fact, the *Digest* will plant an article in a minor magazine if it wants to publish that article.

STAR SYSTEM

- One of our favorite bits of modern journalistic lore is the one that states that the small stars that have appeared on the front cover of *Playboy* magazine—specifically, in and around the P in *Playboy*—reveal the number of times that Hugh Hefner carnally connected with that month's cover girl.

For years the magazine officially explained that the stars were a code to tell advertisers which of a number of regional editions they were looking at. Presumably, a snowmobile advertiser wanted to show up in the one-star midwestern edition, but not in the southwestern five-star edition. The code went up to twelve stars, which were found on the military edition of the magazine.

No matter how many times this was explained in that august forum "The Playboy Advisor," people continued to believe that the stars were directly matched with the vim and pep of Hef's sex life. An Ohio State folkloricist, Harry Joe Jaffe, went so far as to ask a roomful of students to explain the stars. Among the many un-prompted responses were statements as specific as this from an eighteen-year-old decoder: "If appearing on the inside, the star indicates that Hugh Hefner had sex with the girl on the cover. If on the outside, he didn't get any. The number of stars indicates the number of times he tried."

Jaffe reported all of this in *Western Folklore* along with the surprising allegation that Hefner, despite what others in his empire were saying, had helped boost the story. Jaffe quoted this inter-change from an October, 1970, *McCall's* interview as evidence:

> Q: When I was writing an article on the Playboy Club, the girls in the Bunny dressing room said that you didn't like to make love, just to look.
> HEFNER: Well, there's no truth to that at all. Do you know about the stars on the *Playboy* cover? We've got literally hundreds of letters on it. The number of stars near the *P* is supposed to represent the number of times I've had sex with the girl on the cover.

Now all of this has come to an end, as spoilsports at *Playboy* have changed the code. The stars have disappeared from recent issues of the magazine. One of the authors of this book called a *Playboy* executive to find out what had happened to the stars and was told that the code was now secreted away in another part of the cover, but that he would not tell us where. Such is the respect for Ameri-can folklore in the 1980s!

Law

• That whenever a contested will goes to court, the lawyers wind up with most of the money, while the deserving heirs receive little or nothing; this is especially true when the deceased did not have the foresight to leave a written testament.

• That there is such a thing as international law, which, for instance, requires the citizen of one nation to help the citizen of another if that person is floundering in international waters.

• That lawyers employ secret techniques to select jurors apt to be friendly to their causes, to wit:

—Jews and Italians are warmhearted, while Irishmen and some Scandinavians are thought to be colder;

—Women jurors resent attractive women plaintiffs or defendants;

—Former accident victims rarely award another plaintiff more than they received in their own case;

—People in the arts are tolerant, whereas bankers and farmers tend to be conservative.

• That anybody who can read English and follow forms available at any public law library can represent himself in a simple lawsuit. But, just to be safe, you'd better hire a lawyer.

• That even if a lawyer knows his client is guilty, he is professionally obligated to try to persuade the jury otherwise.

• That you can go out and make a "citizen's arrest." This can be done in virtually all circumstances, even when a policeman is caught breaking the law.

• That possession is nine tenths of the law.

• That you can shoot an intruder, trespasser, or adulterer and expect only a slap on the wrist. If you do it in Texas you can forget the slap on the wrist.

• That the most bloodthirsty crimes are often effectively pardoned because minute procedural errors—having nothing to do with guilt or innocence—have been made handling the guilty party.

• That you can legally accuse anyone of anything if you make sure to use the word "alleged."

• That a written contract is absolutely binding and that one who has signed a contract may be forced to do something which he now does not wish to do.

• That the judicial establishment protects its own, which is why the nation must put up with a number of absolutely loony judges.

• That the lawyer who argues the loudest will lose the case because he has decibles, not the law, on his side. (This law is invalid in county seats of less than seventy-five hundred population, and in the courts of Philadelphia, Pennsylvania.)

• That if a witness coughs on the stand, or shifts his eyes around the courtroom, he's lying.

• That you can go out and commit murder and the lawyer can get you free . . . as long as you've got the money.

• That a shyster is the lawyer representing the party on the other side of your lawsuit.

Literature

- That everyone has a life story that would make a good book. All that is needed is for someone to sit down with him and help put it on paper. The movie and paperback money will be divided equally.
- That an author is flattered when you ask to borrow a copy of his book, for it shows you are not a conventional reader who is content to settle for just any copy the book dealer might have on the shelf.
- That an author is further flattered when you state that you are waiting to buy his book in paperback, because you are affirming your faith in his commercial appeal and money-earning potential.
- That an author is flattered when you say you checked out his latest book from the library, because your interest means his library sales should jump immeasurably.
- That authors are indulging in professional pique when they denounce borrowed, paperback, and library books.
- That if you put enough monkeys in front of enough typewriters, it would just be a matter of time before one of them typed *King Lear*.
- That Jules Verne and H. G. Wells predicted virtually all of the inventions and technical trends of the modern era.

- That E. L. Doctorow is a pseudonym for another writer or group of writers.

(Among other versions, it was reported in *The New York Times Book Review* of February 7, 1982, by Edwin McDowell that there were two Doctorow rumors then active in the Southwest: "The first was that the author of *Ragtime* is actually a committee of 'eight ladies,' hence the initials E. L. The other was that the author is a reclusive black doctor whose initials are O. W.; that is, Doctor O. W., or Doctorow.")

- That most bartenders and cabbies could write great books, but never do.

- That writers smoke pipes, wear tweed jackets, and work four and one-half hours a day.

- That many of the female authors of gothic novels are in fact portly, bald, cigar-chomping men.

(Reacting to this credo, the editor of this book, Sandi Gelles-Cole, wrote the authors, "Trust me, many of the female authors of gothic novels are, indeed, rather portly, bald, cigar-chomping men.")

- That there are only (fill in with any number from three to fifteen) basic themes in literature and that every novel and short story you will ever see is a variation on one of the basic themes.

- That the richer the sex life of a writer, the richer his writing.

- That some of the world's greatest novels were never published because the author did not know how to type, and wrote his works in longhand on Indian Chief school pads.

Love, Marriage, and Sex

- That sexual mores are not that much different from the way they were thirty years ago, the main difference being that people talk more about it today.
- That a twenty-three-year-old male is really convincing someone other than himself when he avows he purchases *Playboy* and *Penthouse* magazines for their articles, rather than other features printed as center-folds in living flesh colors.
- That there is love at first sight, that opposites attract, and that absence makes the heart grow fonder.
- That if it had not been for the *National Geographic*, vast numbers of now middle-aged American men would not have known that puberty had begun.
- That June is the luckiest month to get married in.
- That as an area's prostitution and pornography increase, the number of rapes will decline.
- That no one who is married is really happy.
- That no one who is single is really happy.
- That all people who are not married would like to be; that all

unmarried women are looking for a mate; that it is always better for a woman to stay home with her children than to go to work; that it is always a tragedy when a couple divorces; if they have children, it is even worse.

• That a wife never feels truly comfortable with her husband's friends from his bachelor days.

• That southern women are more beautiful than northern women.

• That buxom ladies are less intelligent than those who aren't.

• That pretty girls smile back at old men just because they wish to make them feel good; actually, they are interested, and are dying to make the age-jump if asked (but they never are).

• That women can withstand colder temperatures because of additional "fatty tissue"; and that women are not the weaker sex because they typically outlive men.

• That bras were burned during the early days of the modern women's movement.

(Quoting Ellen Goodman, "Someday when they write a media history of the women's movement, the chapter on the 1970s will be called 'The Bra-Burning That Never Happened.' This will focus on the nationwide report of the Flaming Feminists who set a torch to their underwear. In fact, no piece of lingerie was ever kindled in anger, but from then on, women's rights advocates were permanently labeled 'bra-burners.' " Ms. Goodman to the contrary, one of the authors witnessed, in a reportorial capacity, a conflagration fueled by bras at a demonstration on the Atlantic City boardwalk outside the Democratic National Convention in August 1964.)

• That a symptom of pregnancy is a craving for ice cream and pickles.

• That primitive women have a much easier time in childbirth than their sisters in more developed cultures.

• That men have one less rib than women.

- That lesbians always wear short hair.
- That most teen-agers have only a vague notion of what sex is, and no inclination to try it unless they've had a sex education class.
- That in women sexual enjoyment is directly correlated with education; hence the more educated a woman, the more frequently she experiences orgasm. Uneducated women, conversely, never enjoy orgasm. (Sociologist Lynn Eden, responsible for this credo, says persons in her profession call this a "spurious variable," i.e., bunk.)
- That unusually high numbers of children are born at the time of the full moon.

(Despite studies to the contrary, this belief is still widely held, especially among nurses, who should know better. For reasons unclear, professionals often err on the side of mythology, e.g., police officers who insist that that the worst human behavior is displayed under a full moon.)

- That an abnormally high number of babies are born nine months from the time of a power outage, blackout, or evening when normal TV programing is preempted by news.

(In *More Misinformation,* Tom Burnam reports that a study of the effects of the New York blackout of 1965 showed a slight decrease.)

- That women who ride horses are oversexed.
- That a small, but nonetheless significant, percentage of the people who are walking the streets are there because of drugstore clerks who, with pins, poked holes in condom packages.
- That people with particularly active sex lives tend to have extra energy to apply to other pursuits. That people whose sex lives are inactive tend to have extra energy to apply to other pursuits.
- That homosexuals are uniformly creative and graceful and are hardly ever dullards.
- That heterosexual males are generally clumsy.
- That extremely handsome men tend to be gay.
- That there are very few blue-collar homosexuals.

That a small, but nonetheless significant, percentage of the people who are walking the streets are there because of drugstore clerks who, with pins, poked holes in condom packages.

- That homosexuals recognize one another with a single glance, because of recognition signals inexplicable to the straight world.
- That the sex life of a homosexual is akin to that of the most popular girl in a Las Vegas brothel.
- That you can always tell a gay male by the way he dresses; that gay men are more fashionable; that gay men love clothes in order to compensate for unhappy lives; that gay clones are as conformist (macho, antirevolutionary, woman-hating) as their clothing.

(Jeff Weinstein, who regularly writes about gay affairs for *The Village Voice,* cites these "credos" under what he regards as their more proper designation—he calls them "four lies about gay male fashion.")

Military

- That the Air Force could teach apes to fly but couldn't make them salute.
- That the Navy has a ten-day supply of any necessary item, such as fuel or ordnance, and a fifty-year supply of oyster forks for the officers' mess.
- That the armed forces of the United States have and will always make colossal mistakes in assignments—for example, assigning trombonists to tank repair and putting mechanics in the Army band.
- That the Pentagon has spent billions of taxpayer dollars on mindless research projects having to do with the dynamics of yo-yos, the masturbatory habits of elk, and the use of agricultural metaphor in Icelandic folklore.
- That the Air Force has discovered the true nature of UFOs but is keeping it secret in the interest of national security.
- That there are no atheists in foxholes.
- That whoever controls the Indian Ocean controls the world.
- That the brass at the Pentagon routinely substitute sea gull for chicken in mess halls.

• That there is a hidden ward of World War I, World War II, Korean, and Vietnam War veterans at Walter Reed which is so gruesome that nurses who are assigned there go crazy after a year and have to be treated at a special hospital out West.

• This is adjacent to the 450-bed facility that the Catholic Church maintains to dry out alcoholic priests. Just over the hill is the CIA's "sex camp," where vacationing covert agents can enjoy feminine companionship without fear of compromise.

• Four thousand miles to the west is the island where the Marine Corps permanently quarantined the hardened killers it did not dare return to the U.S. after the Second World War. They have Polynesian wives and unlimited supplies of Schlitz beer.

• That because there is on occasion reference to death and devastation, *M*A*S*H* gives us a pretty good idea of what the Korean War was really like.

• That every successful military unit has an innovative supply sergeant who can start out with a dented canteen and trade his way upward to two carloads of steaks and a tanker of beer.

Nationalities

- That if a foreigner in America cannot speak English, he lacks a certain amount of intelligence. However, the reverse is not true of an American abroad.
- That Americans have the highest standard of living in the world.

(Measuring the "highest" or "best" standard of living is a highly subjective undertaking; one of the authors insists that statistical evidence notwithstanding, the Shenandoah Valley of Virginia offers more amenities than any locale on earth. Measuring the quality of life is a highly subjective undertaking involving more factors than the cash available to a citizen. But on the dollar scale, Kuwait in 1978 had the highest gross national product per person, $15,970, compared to $12,299 for Switzerland, $9,770 for the U.S., and $5,720 for Britain. Kuwait's riches have not enhanced its appeal for the average citizen.)

- That it is always a shame when the third generation of American-born descendants of someone from the Old Country speaks only English, knows no ethnic dances, and would rather go to Disney World than to the Old Country to visit distant cousins who speak no English and live in grubby little towns with no indoor toilets.

- That something insidious is tearing at the fabric of American life, which is made evident by the contract demands of professional athletes and the behavior of rock stars.
- That the average American is a wellspring of common sense and is never hoodwinked for long.
- That any American believes he can perform three tasks better than the people who are currently doing them: teach school, govern the state, and edit the local newspaper.
- That if a person doesn't speak very good English, you must shout at him to be understood.
- That millions of people in this world dream of having their picture taken by an American tourist with a Polaroid camera.
- That most French-Canadian women are named Marie.
- That most Mexican women are named Maria.
- That the average European has better taste than the average American.
- That English lords are wastrels and drink too much port; when they open their estates to the public for fee-tours, however, they can be charming and out-of-the-mold.
- That French is a pretty language and German an ugly one.
- That despite their many graces, the French are incredibly rude to Americans, especially if they are trying to speak French with less than perfect fluency.
- That Germans and Japanese work harder than Americans.
- That the only watch worth owning comes from Switzerland.
- That the average Swiss is trilingual, thrifty, and politically neutral.
- That the Danes and Norwegians have never forgiven the Swedes for their neutrality during World War II.
- That Swedes are sullen, sexually promiscuous, and suicidal.
- That the Irish say "Begorra," Swedes "Yumpin' Yiminey,"

WOULD YOU GENTLY INFORM THE PONTIFF THAT DO TO A COMMUNICATIONS ERROR... UH, ...HE'S INVESTED 2 MILLION IN CONDOMS, NOT CONDOMINIUMS. UH, HELLO?

That the Vatican has huge (but unspecified) commercial holdings in the U. S.

French *"Sacrebleu,"* Germans *"Was ist das?"* etcetera, whenever they have nothing better to say.

• That the Russians are an artless, clumsy crew except when it comes to the ballet.

• That your average Russian is a fine person who adores the average American. Russian leaders, on the other hand, are hatemongers who never miss a chance to say something nasty about the U.S.A.

• That a Russian would gladly hand over six months' wages and his firstborn child for a pair of Levi's jeans, a carton of Kents, and a UCLA sweat shirt.

• That all American tourists visiting the Soviet Union are bugged in their hotel rooms by the KGB, who dutifully study every word.

• That despite their fits of indignation when they hear Polish jokes, Poles secretly enjoy the attention.

• That Chinese inscrutability is a constant.

• That the Chinese people are fanatically honest and that all Americans who have visited there (whether it was 1920 or 1980) return

associated with formalized education, although things do tend to get a bit noisy at times.

•   That as long as parents drink martinis and smoke cigarettes, they have no legitimate say regarding the habits of their fourteen-year-old children.

•   That the powerful and venal tobacco lobby is behind all those bogus studies showing that marijuana is bad for youngsters.

•   That the tobacco companies have already registered the names "Colombian Red" and "Acapulco Yellow" in preparation for their domination of the marijuana market once sales of the weed are legalized.

•   That the sexually liberated tend toward greater compassion.

•   That ethnic jokes show how liberated we really are from racial stereotyping, and are therefore a sign of health. However, best be careful what you say around a Polish or black linebacker from the NFL.

•   That an individual human being's character, personality, and daily destiny are all preordained by the position of the stars and the planets at the exact moment of birth.

•   That corporate profits are *obscene* but that the sleaziest offerings of a porno shop are not.

•   That the American family is disintegrating.

•   That each long-distance telephone call consumes enough energy to mean the death of three flowers somewhere in the world.

•   That turning on a light switch consumes more electricity than if you had left the lamp on for fifteen minutes while you were out of the room. Ditto for the ignition of a car.

•   That if you are not part of the solution, you are part of the problem.

Physical

Characteristics

- That a soft voice is a sign of good breeding in a man.
- That a firm handshake is a sign of honesty; that a weak handshake means the person is suspicious and should be watched; that a damp handshake is a sign of nervousness.
- That if a short man is aggressive, it's because he is so short; if he is not, it's because he is so short.
- That there are some people who cannot wear watches because of some mysterious bodily effect that causes them to stop.
- That "spread" is the inevitable consequence of middle age. (As both authors would concede under cross-examination, blaming "spread" on middle age is a rationalization for not exercising or eating properly.)
- That a strong back and weak mind are just as surely paired as a strong mind and a weak back.
- That a square jaw is a sign of determination in a person.
- That slender hands signify artistic ability.
- That bushy eyebrows are a certain sign of sexuality in a male;

That early shaving encourages more rapid beard growth.

that long fingers hint at a related development; that a woman who constantly licks her lips is deserving of special attention.

• That blondes have more fun, tan better, and are generally dumber.

• That brunettes are more trustworthy than blondes.

• That redheads have quick and violent tempers.

• That early shaving encourages more rapid beard growth.

• That a hairy chest is a sign of strength.

• That black skin gives greater protection against sunburn and heat prostration.

(In his 1946 book *The Natural History of Nonsense,* Bergen Evans eloquently states, ". . . the belief that the Negro is 'equipped' to endure heat better than the white man serves to distract attention from the fact that he is not. Millions of Negroes work long hours in the hot sun for others' profit, and it is easier and cheaper for the others to believe that the Negroes 'just naturally don't mind' than it would be to provide shorter hours, rest periods, and cool drinking water. Yet, contrary to general belief, the pigmentation of their skin affords them no great protection from sunburn or heat prostration." Evans went on to cite life insurance statistics that showed that two to six times as many blacks were dying from heat as whites.)

• That you should not trust anyone with one long eyebrow.

• That if you pull a gray hair out of your head, a dozen more will grow in its place.

• That any male who wears a short haircut works for IBM, the FBI, or is a Marine.

• That shifty-eyed people are more likely to be dishonest than those with a fixed gaze.

(From a 1977 Associated Press dispatch: "There is no connection between eye-gaze fixity and honesty. On the contrary, one study showed

that, compared with normal persons, psychopathic liars actually main-
tained steadier eye contact in speaking with others.")

•   That shaving makes hair grow in faster and thicker.
(The rate of hair growth is predetermined by hereditary factors and
shaving or not shaving will have no effect on the rate of growth.)

•   That big ears are a sign of generosity, while small ears denote
a stingy person. A 'big head little wit, little head not a bit.' A high brow
denotes noble character and a low one stupidity. A man with close-set
eyes is mean, while one with a long nose or crossed eyes has a cranky
disposition. A long chin signifies jealousy, and large lips indicate a
grouch. Buck teeth indicate a tattler. If a man's eyebrows meet, he is
sure to have a fiery disposition.

•   That a wide and bald forehead is a sign of genius. That too lush
a beard or an excess of body hair encourages baldness.

•   That men with beards are hiding something (or hiding from
something).

•   That you can judge the size of a man's organ by the size of his
nose or thumb.

•   That fat women always have good skin and pretty faces.

•   That any person, regardless of prominence or outward poise, has
a secret Achilles' heel that is shielded from the public.
(In truth, some may have two Achilles' heels, others none.)

Politics

•   That Congress and the government exist to serve big business and special interests, but nobody will admit it. They camouflage the fact with patriotic rhetoric about "the will of the people and the good of the country," disguise it with spurious studies and rigged investigations, or cover it up with official falsehoods. It is safer to believe nothing than to believe a politician or the government.

•   That Congress would be so much more effective if it were not for the fact that it is overloaded with lawyers.

•   That politicians aren't crooked until after their first term in office.

•   That five hundred people pulled off the street at random would run the nation as well as Congress—and get into less trouble.

•   That an incumbent President is always reelected if the closing Dow Jones industrial average is higher the Monday before the election than it was on the opening day of the election year.

(If this old axiom were true, Jimmy Carter would have been reelected in 1980—the average on election eve was 937.20, up from 824.57 on the year's first day of trading.

- That high-quality American political leadership is a thing of the past.
- That politics makes strange bedfellows.

(Upon examination, even the oddest of political alliances usually has an underlying rationale; i.e., bootleggers in the South long made common cause with ministers in support of laws prohibiting liquor sales, the first group motivated by profit, the second by theology.)

- That only Republican administrations can reach agreement with communist nations because Democratic administrations are always fearful the GOP will bait them with accusations of being "soft on communism."
- That politicians with whom you disagree have sold out to big business, big labor, and/or other special-interest groups, whereas politicians who share your views reached their conclusions by carefully weighing the issues.
- That generals make lousy Presidents. But in retrospect, Eisenhower wasn't all that bad.
- That there are secret basement hideways in Congressional office buildings in which members indulge in drinking binges and sexual orgies during lunch hour, which extends from eleven thirty A.M. until four thirty P.M., and that capitol police are chosen on the understanding they will look the other way.
- That the Presidency of the U.S. is too big a job for one man.
- That advocating gun control consumes enough psychic energy to send a 1948 Hudson to the moon and beyond, and with about as much purpose.
- That—despite 1980—there is a great Kennedy organization that is hidden but which will emerge as a powerful force when the time is right.

(In 1979 columnist John P. Roche termed this the "most indestructible myth in American politics.")

• That if the TV networks kept their cameras on the nonsense of the podium for an entire political convention, viewers would turn to game shows and movie reruns. That by the second night of an uncontested convention, most people do so anyway.

• That the war would have been over in six months if we'd elected Goldwater. Or McCarthy. Or Humphrey. Or McGovern. Or Wallace.

• That if all the people who *say* that they did not vote for Nixon actually did not vote for Nixon, he never would have been elected President.

• That the President of the United States must possess a large dog, on the scale of an Irish setter, to be an effective Chief Executive.

• That the President must be a member of a church and attend its public ceremonies regularly.

• That regardless of what services he might be performing to better the Republic, a Vice-President of the United States must be viewed with the condescension one reserves for an unemployed brother-in-law, or the neighborhood crank. That each new President avows his Vice-President is to have a significant policy-making role in the administration, a vow that has been known to last as long as three weeks. That an intelligent politician consults the actuarial tables before accepting the nomination for Vice-President.

• That Democrats squabble like a roomful of wet cats at their national political conventions, but always manage to unite by November and win (except in those years when they don't and lose).

• That the quality of a speech to a Democratic National Convention is gauged by the number of references to the "revered and great" former Presidents Roosevelt, Truman, Kennedy, and Johnson; the more skilled orators pause after each name to provide space for clapping. The harder hitters take a swipe at Herbert Hoover, even though graybeards have to explain his significance to younger delegates.

• That the banalities of political convention speeches should be forgiven because no one expects anything else from the party hacks chosen to deliver them.

- That Democrats aren't all that bad, once you sit down and have a drink with them.
- That Republicans aren't all that bad, once you sit down and have a drink with them.
- That you shouldn't talk politics or religion with strangers at a party.

Professional

- That all dentists have hairy arms.
- That preachers' sons never amount to anything and that their daughters are sexually active at age fifteen.

(This has been an American credo for generations. Several major studies have been made to see if there is any truth to this supposition, including one by Havelock Ellis, who concluded that "eminent children of the clergy considerably outnumber those of lawyers, doctors, and army officers put together.")

- That cabdrivers know secret routes, based mainly upon back alleys and other secondary thoroughfares, that get them across Washington, or midtown New York, twice as fast as you could in your own car; that most drivers are Archie Bunker prototypes, but you listen to them anyway as keen barometers of public opinion, especially on the subjects of office-holders, civil rights, and municipal highway improvement programs.

(Passengers in taxicabs, particularly out-of-town journalists, frequently mistake garrulity for wisdom.)

- That there is a driver in Cleveland, or maybe Toledo, who speaks only in response to direct questions. We think.
- That truckers always help motorists in distress.

- That there are no blond morticians.
- That an ability to quote the Scripture enhances a minister's expertise at saving sinners from eternal damnation, and makes him a more credible figure to his lodge brothers.
- That admirals flounder in twelve-foot sailboats and astronauts are all thumbs when it comes to piloting light planes.
- That great mathematicians cannot balance their own checkbooks, stockbrokers tend to bet heavily on horse races, chefs rely on convenience foods at home, and doctors often overlook less-than-major illness and injury in their own homes.

FARMER'S CREDOS

- That carrying a buckeye in one's pocket will ward off arthritis and head colds.
- That leaving the carcass of a coyote or a crow on a fence will dissuade the appearance of other predators.
- That thunder will sour fresh milk.
(The sudden temperature changes associated with thunderstorms give this credo a surface credibility.)
- That brokers on the Chicago commodity exchanges make far more from each year's crops than the farmers who actually grow them.
- That hogs should not be butchered until first frost.
(Again, a credo linked to the weather: cool temperatures mean less chance of meat spoiling during dressing.)
- That leaving a small portion of food on one's plate after each meal ensures that the plate will never be empty during the coming year.

Psychology

- That many cases of mental illness could be prevented if people would only take a little time to "get hold of themselves."
- That you can't change human nature.
- That people who are crazy or off balance become more so when there is a full moon.

(Despite the fact that this has been disproven in studies that look at such things as the relative number of people admitted to mental hospitals during periods when the moon is full, the belief persists.)

- That psychiatrists' children are always in need of a psychiatrist (just as shoemakers' children have holes in their shoes).
- That therapists have more problems than their patients, and that female clients are convinced that seduction on the couch is the only route to a swift cure.

(This has, of course, happened, but on nothing approaching the scale it reaches in popular legend.)

- That you can be hypnotized against your will.
- That bright people are more likely to have nervous breakdowns than dull ones.

- That the holiday season brings on depression in large numbers of people.

(Ohio State University psychiatrist Stephen Pariser has studied the phenomenon of holiday depression and concluded that it is a creation of the media and that there is little evidence to support the contention that depression is any greater in December than in July.)

- That many persons come away from their consultations feeling that the psychiatrist is nuttier than they are. He sometimes is.

- That people who talk of committing suicide never do.

Regional

• That any given New England farmer has more common sense than a Harvard professor. This holds true as well for Texas shrimp fishermen, New York cabdrivers, and bricklayers in Seattle, Washington.

• That if you prowl the back roads of rural New England, you will chance across small inns run by hospitable couples who serve four-star meals, provide comfortable featherbed rooms with a fireplace, and send you on the way in the morning with a country breakfast and a smile, for less than twenty dollars. Unfortunately, these places are never pinpointed in guidebooks.

• That all small New England towns are in possession of at least one haunted house, one Indian legend, and the mortal remains of an early patriot.

• That to the diehard Yankees of northern New England everything south of Hartford is the Deep South; that to the apartment dwellers of Manhattan there is nothing to the west of the Hudson River save open range and an occasional used-car lot, and that a Texan's view of the rest of the nation is of a right and left coast that run just beyond either side of Oklahoma.

• That citizens in the eastern United States have a keen interest in forest fires in remote regions of the American West, a curiosity understood and fulfilled by the persons who produce hourly newscasts on the radio networks.

• That there is, to this day, a community of women in the southern states, naturally generations removed from direct involvement in the Civil War, whose lives are marked by passionate, overwhelming hatred of Yankees.

(These women are not to be confused with female Boston Red Sox fans, whose lives are similarly marked.)

• That southern cold feels colder than northern cold.

• That southerners go into a catatonic trance at the smell of fried chicken, or the sound of Johnny Cash's voice. That all of Dixie spends Saturday night either listening to the Grand Ole Opry on the radio or watching a demolition derby. That every small southern town contains an intelligent and quietly liberal lawyer who is "sensible" on the racial issue and thus a credit to his race when written about in eastern journals.

• That the Rocky Mountain states are populated by two kinds of people: mellow young environmentalists who always wear plaid shirts and jeans and know John Denver personally, and old-timers with faces as craggy as the mountains.

• That southern California contains all the off-the-wall nuts and that northern California (as well as Washington and Oregon) is an Olympian, conservative, cultivated place, managed well by a few old families.

• That there is no body of beliefs so bizarre that it does not have an active cult following in the southwest corner of the nation.

Rich People,

Poor People, Etc.

- That all urban bag ladies went to Vassar, Wellesley, or Bryn Mawr.
- That all inherited wealth represents Grandpa's ill-gotten gains; that all rich people are unhappy; that all rich people marry five times and raise miserable children because they don't know the secret of a happy life, which is readily obtainable from any passing factory worker.
- That all persons of great wealth or responsibility secretly pine for the simple life.
- That the poor waste whatever money they get hold of, thereby preventing them from entry into the middle class.
- That the rural poor are somehow less miserable than the urban poor.
- That illiterate people sign their names by making large, crude X's.
- That the people who were most popular in high school amount to nothing in later life. The "nerds" from high school become highly successful.

- That people who get up early are of generally better character than those who get up late.
- That silent people tend to be deep thinkers.
- That pipe smokers are lousy tippers and deliberate excessively when making a purchase.
- That primitive people have good teeth and cannot get lost in the wilderness.
- That a single migrant farm worker, or parking lot attendant, can save enough money in a year to support his entire Latin American village through the 1980s; how he performs such fiscal ingenuity on an hourly wage of $3.10 is now under study by the learned dons of Harvard University.
- That there are thousands of safety deposit boxes in banks around the country crammed full of cash and jewelry left by long-deceased actors and eccentrics; if converted to public use, these riches would reduce the income tax by upwards of fifteen percent.
- That despite what sociologists, journalists, and others have reported, there are great numbers of Americans who are quite content with dull, repetitive, and demeaning jobs.
- That every prediction told by a fortune teller includes the admonition to beware of tall, dark strangers, and the forecast that travel is in one's future.
- That members of the Masonic order are taught mysterious, secret rituals; that any Mason who divulges these secrets dies suddenly and mysteriously; that the letter G in the Masonic emblem refers to the use of a goat in certain of the order's rituals.
- That if the total wealth of the United States were equally divided among all citizens, five years thereafter we would be back to the same unequal division we have now, with control of the wealth in largely the same hands as today.

Science, Technology, and Nature

- That new technology always takes five years to develop; the only exception being during World War II, when things were developed and put into production and service almost overnight.
- That perpetual motion is a goal worth striving for, as it will bring about great benefits to mankind.
- That at some indefinite point in the future we will live in energy-efficient domed solar cities, move about on monorails, and wear togas.
- That the main earthly effect of the space program has been to change the weather.
- That scientists are motivated by a search for the truth, except for those involved in technology, who are only interested in the buck.
- That if you make a statistical sample large enough, it will be right.
- That there are an infinite number of ways of using statistics as a means to deceive.
- That the eventual solutions to the problems of the aged, handicapped, and poor will come from Space Age technology.

• That computers do not make errors. That only humans make computer errors.

• That American science and technology only get moving when posed with an outside threat (Pearl Harbor, Sputnik, the Arab oil embargo).

• That warm water freezes faster than cold water.

• That it is possible to divine for water with a forked willow branch. If, however, the dip of the branch indicates an area that is dry, it only means that the divining was done improperly or by an inexperienced diviner.

• That moss only grows on the north side of trees.

• That if you hold a seashell to your ear you can hear the roar of the ocean. You should bring at least a dozen shells home each time you visit the shore.

(The sound you hear actually comes from sounds around you that are picked up and intensified in the inner spaces of the shell.)

• That it is possible for the average person to get a poinsettia to bloom for a second Christmas.

Show Business

- That a single negative review in *The New York Times* can kill a Broadway show after one night; that if the *Times* had been around to review Shakespeare, English teachers would be teaching another playwright today.
- That a cabal of five advertising executives dictates the content of prime-time viewing on the three major networks. They are fearful that new ideas might disturb viewers; hence the repetitive quality of what Americans are forced to watch.
- That when a television program breaks for a commercial, the volume becomes perceptibly higher than that of the regular program.
- That cable television has vast but unspecified potential to deliver us more than six-month-old box-office flops, commercial-free reruns of *Life of Riley*, and Atlanta Hawks games.
- That people who claim that they only watch documentaries on television never miss an episode of *Dukes of Hazzard*, *Magnum, P.I.*, or *Three's Company*.
- That radio editorials are better than commercials, but not by enough to make one wish to listen to them more than once or so weekly.

• That a number of female movie stars of the period from approximately 1930 through 1960 were discovered at the counter of Schwab's Pharmacy at Sunset Boulevard and Laurel.

• That not too long ago a few minutes of a most graphic X-rated movie was accidentally shown on prime-time television in another city.

(This story dates back to the time when X-rated movies were called "stag movies" and is always told about a city well outside the teller's viewing area. However, the very morning one of the authors read this credo in galley form, newscaster Paul Harvey reported just such an event the previous evening in Las Vegas, involving the interruption of *Love Boat* by eleven seconds of porn.)

• That it is bad luck to wish an actor good luck.

• That in defiance of the nutritional laws governing the health of more mundane mortals, rock stars can subsist indefinitely on a diet of cocaine and M&M candies. Most of them, however, come to tragic ends at an early age, and remain alive as immortals in their fans' memories for as long as three weeks.

• That if you listen closely to the subliminal sounds in Beatles recordings, you can gain insight into such happenings as the results of future presidential elections, the gold market, and the origins of man.

• That if you are a man and are going to appear on TV you should wear a blue shirt (never a white one.)

• That the only westerns worth watching are *Stagecoach* and *High Noon.*

• That all jokes heard on *The Tonight Show,* in Las Vegas lounges, at last week's PTA meeting, or wherever derive from *Joe Miller's Jests* of 1739.

• That bad times are best for the movie business, as people throng to adventures and musicals to forget their problems.

• That all film stars and rock stars live miserable, dissipated lives, until they either (1) commit suicide or (2) are baptized in Pat Boone's pool. If (2), they then take menial jobs and thank God their wretched success is behind them.

• That utterly fascinating and fantastic conversations take place in the "green rooms" of television talk shows, which are interrupted so that less interesting conversations can take place in front of the camera.

• That the world's leading pop songs occur to the composer while he is showering or making love, and are converted into final-score form within twenty minutes or so.

• That in order to amount to anything as a comedian in America you must either have been born in Brooklyn or in a small town in the Midwest.

• That good conversation, especially among families, has been drowned out by television. (This replaces the belief that it was drowned out by radio, which replaces the belief that it was drowned out by the stereoscope.)

Space

- That humans would be incapable of dealing with beings from elsewhere in space and the yahoos among us would shoot them on sight if they ever landed on earth.
- That there are canals on Mars.
- That NASA has discovered the existence of a "lost day" but is hiding the fact from the public.

(This belief is so widely held that the Space Agency includes the following disclaimer in "This is NASA," the basic pamphlet it uses to describe its activities: "There is no truth to the recurring story that NASA uncovered a 'lost day' in the movement of the Earth. Although planetary positions are used to help determine spacecraft orbits, we have been unable to learn of any computations in the space program which revealed a 'lost day,' as has been reported in a number of places.")

- That it was easier to land astronauts on the moon than it is to cleanse a polluted river.
- That the National Aeronautics and Space Administration has made unimagined discoveries that it is now hiding for fear of widespread panic.

• That most of the people who report UFO sightings live in or near swamps and seldom comb their hair. That if a Ph.D. scientist sees a UFO he is immediately given a large "grant" from the Air Force or National Security Agency in exchange for his silence.

That most of the people who report UFO sightings live in or near swamps and seldom comb their hair.

Sports

- That tennis balls contain poisonous gas.
- That an athlete should not engage in sex the night before a big game.
- That Abner Doubleday invented baseball and that it was first played in Cooperstown, New York.

(The Doubleday myth stemmed in part from the desire of the early pooh-bahs of baseball to prove that their sport was American in origin. Among other points that have been made in disproving the myth is that Doubleday was at West Point when he was supposedly in Cooperstown inventing the game. In fact, there is no proof that he was *ever* in Cooperstown. It actually evolved from English cricket and rounders as well as other hybrid American games of the early 1800s.)

- That if a baseball pitcher is working on a no-hitter, no mention should be made of it lest he be jinxed.
- That any male American knows how to keep score at a baseball game; he knows the fine points of all the rules of all major American sports and can explain them to his wife, who won't understand them anyway.

That tennis balls contain poisonous gas.

• That it is a great and noble thing for a man to take his son to a baseball game.

• That a baseball player whose sensational play provides the third out in an inning is always the leadoff hitter when his team comes to bat.

• That even when the Chicago Cubs won their last pennant in 1945, it wasn't worth much, since all but the halt and the lame were at war.

• That the people who make baseball cards hold back on super-stars so that in order to get a Dave Winfield or Pete Rose you have to buy five nobodies from the Cubs or Mariners.

• That boxing is still the surest and fastest ticket from poverty to fame and fortune.

• That a city with a winning National Football League team loses 7.1 hours work time weekly per capita in water-cooler discussions about the last and next week's game.

That from time to time a golfer who will not leave the links despite the imminence of an electrical storm will be hit by lightning.

- That a city with a losing National Football League team loses 7.1 hours weekly per capita in water-cooler discussions about the last and next week's games.
- That cities without National Football League teams are populated by men who lose 7.1 hours weekly in water-cooler discussions about the local high school or college season.
- That quarterbacks and even offensive guards in the National Football League keep in their heads intricate plays and assignments that are beyond the comprehension of Princeton mathematicians; once off the field, however, they must read cue cards to get through beer commercials.
- That the best football players come from Texas or Pennsylvania.
- That significant numbers of American men do away with themselves on the Sunday afternoons just after the Super Bowl.
- That a number of our leading stock-car drivers learned how to drive from running corn liquor and evading revenuers on mountain roads.

(The kernel of truth behind this credo is the fact that Junior Johnson, crew manager for Cale Yarborough, Darrell Waltrip, and other champions of the National Association of Stock Car Auto Racing—in fact, served time in a Federal prison for hauling moonshine.)

- That if you are having a great day fishing and decide to stop and count your catch, your luck will evaporate and you will be fortunate to catch even one more.
- That fish only bite at sunset and dawn.
- That one can draw successfully to fill an inside straight.
- That if you are lucky at cards you will be unlucky in love.
- That a backwoods logger or big-bellied trucker is the worth of several karate experts in a fight.
- That the basketball player to make the last basket during warmup will have a good game.

That "close" counts only in horseshoes.

• That from time to time a golfer who will not leave the links despite the imminence of an electrical storm will be hit by lightning. The intrepid golfer will be unharmed, but his clubs will melt.

• That when teeing off in golf you should place the ball so that the brand name is up. If it is not up, you will lose the hole.

• That South American soccer fans are an irrational, temperamental lot—unlike the people who go to watch American college and professional football.

• That "close" counts only in horseshoes.

• That chess is excellent discipline for the mind—far superior to television or reading.

• That the America's Cup race is an exciting event provided you understand all the nuances of sailing.

• That people who can water-ski find it easy to snow-ski; and the reverse.

• That jogging is beneficial both physically and spiritually, and any day now we are going to give it a try; that anyone past age thirty-five should consult a physician before undertaking so strenuous a sport, and that next week, or maybe the next, we intend to ask the doctor about it; that in the interim we are reading a book by Jack Kennedy's back doctor on the health-enhancing qualities of rocking chairs.

• That the Baby Ruth candy bar was named for slugger Babe Ruth.

(Actually it was named for President Grover Cleveland's daughter Ruth.)

• That a team or individual athlete will by jinxed during the week they appear on the cover of *Sports Illustrated.*

• That it's not the heat that gets to you, it's the humidity.

• That there are people who can predict the weather by paying attention to their corns, their lumbago, or some other bodily forecaster.

• That lightning never strikes twice in the same place.

(According to the *Chicago Tribune* the Empire State Building was struck forty-eight times in a single year.)

• That when smoke from a chimney lies close to the ground, it will either rain or snow.

• That a moon is responsible for changes in the weather.

• That no matter what the forecast says, a newly washed car will cause it to rain.

• That if you leave your umbrella at home, it is sure to rain.

• That the hue of the sky is a more accurate warning of nautical weather conditions than is the weather service, to wit:

> Red sky at night,
> Sailors delight.
> Red sky at morning,
> Sailors take warning.

The Great Ineradicable Modern Fable

In the spring of 1961 one of the authors received an anguished telephone
call from a colleague who reported on police matters for *The Dallas
Morning News.* His information seemed solid, for it had been told to the
publisher at a cocktail party only the evening before by an esteemed
banker. Nonetheless, the police reporter could find no verifying details.
Did the story perhaps fall within the jurisdiction of the author, who at
that time was monitoring happenings of the Dallas County Sheriff's
Department for news of sociological and historical importance? The
outline was as follows:

Several days earlier a man's car had stalled on the Central Expressway.
He'd waved his arm for assistance, and a woman motorist had stopped.
He explained that he thought a brief push would make his vehicle
operative again and admonished, "But you must get up to about thirty-
five miles an hour to do any good." The woman had nodded assent, and
the man had returned to his car.

He'd waited, and waited, and fidgeted, and eventually glanced into his
rearview mirror. There the woman was, bearing down on him in her car
at thirty-five miles an hour.

As the police reporter explained, "The city cops don't have any record of any stalled-car accident on Central Expressway. I thought maybe it could have happened on Central in the sheriff's jurisdiction."

Well, it hadn't, as a desk sergeant stated with a guffaw when queried. "That one comes along every six months," he said. "Last time it was on Stemmons Freeway. That time the second driver was a French tourist at forty-five miles an hour."

Several months later the coauthor shifted journalistic duty stations to *The Philadelphia Inquirer.* Soon after his arrival the city editor bustled over with a grin and a page of notes. "The darnedest thing happened on the Schuylkill Expressway the other night," he said. "It seems this guy's car stalled, and . . ."

You know what else he said. Word of mouth, surely a means of communication challenging in swiftness a laser beam, had a new urban legend to disseminate around the country. Soon it would join the bathing suit that became transparent (an embarrassment that earned either $10,000 or $55,000 or $125,000 in damages for a woman in either Michigan, Florida, or Oregon, in a proceeding that somehow was never recorded in court records), the mouse in the pop bottle, and the black widow spider that built a nest in a woman's beehive hairdo (or was it in a hippie's unshorn locks?) and bit and killed her.

That a story is of unverifiable authenticity—a roundabout way of saying it smells to high heaven—does not restrain Americans from relishing and retelling it with their own variations—and, who knows, even coming to accept it as a valid vignette of modern society. As a wizard whose name is lost to recorded history once remarked, "Never let the truth get in the way of a good story." Jan Harold Brunvand, of the University of Utah, offered a definition for the "modern urban legend" in his book *The Study of American Folklore.* He called such legends "contemporary stories in a city setting which are reported as true individual experiences, but which have traditional variants that indicate their legendary character."

Urban legends survive for years, to die out and then suddenly reappear. A story has currency, and supposed validity, then is told so often and with so many variations that it becomes suspect, and is discarded. "The Concrete-Filled Car" is an off-again, on-again classic. Angry with his wife because of suspected infidelities, the driver of a cement transport truck happens past the house one afternoon and sees the lover's car parked outside. He rolls down its windows and fills the car with three tons of wet cement. (This is the southern/southwestern variant; in eastern states the aggrieved husband drives a fuel-oil truck; his solution is equally messy.) Sometimes this story is embellished with a kicker. The car, usually a Cadillac, is a surprise birthday present for the cement-truck driver and the man in the house is the salesman delivering the title and getting his check.

By the way, many of these stories are international. A friend of ours reports that the cement-truck story is making the rounds in Sweden.

The long-running modern urban fable has several, if not all, of the following qualities, which contribute to its survival:

I.   It contains a semblance of seemingly supportive specific detail.

The woman tries on a parka imported from Hong Kong, priced at $29.95, at a department store in a specific shopping plaza outside Hackensack, New Jersey. A viper nesting in the lining fatally bites her. Other coats are ripped apart; each is found to contain one or more vipers. An "authority on snakes" from the National Zoo in Washington comes to the scene and declares that a "mother viper" apparently laid eggs in a pile of kapok used for the lining. Despite an attempted hush-up, word of the tragedy leaks out from the sister of an intern who was on duty at the hospital emergency room when the dying woman was brought in. None of the principals cited, of course, knows anything about any such incident—nor do they when it occurs again in Washington, D.C., in December 1969, and the following spring in Dallas. A budding folklorist could probably build a reputation just recording the variations on this one theme: "It was actually in a pile of sweaters from Taiwan." . . . "What I heard was, the woman wasn't dead but was in a coma and the department store has spent thousands to keep it hushed up."

Incidentally, when *The Washington Star*'s Woody West refuted the snake story in 1969 ("How the Public Was Snake-Bitten by a Rumor"), he found that his paper had gone through a lengthy investigation refuting still another snake story in the summer of 1940. Back then there was a tenacious rumor going around that a woman had been bitten by a snake at an amusement park.

II.   The person who retells the yarn accepts its validity because of the source from which it comes.

A reputable journalist hears policemen in a suburban Philadelphia town laughing among themselves and is told a you-can't-print-this story. The previous evening the wife of a prominent Main Line financier hears a noise downstairs. She arouses her husband. Nude, he goes downstairs and finds water dripping into a pan beneath the sink. He bends over to investigate. The family cat happens by and takes a friendly swipe at the man's rear (or private parts). Startled, the financier arises, bumps his head, and falls to the floor unconscious. The wife telephones the police and ambulance; before they arrive, the husband awakes and tells her what happened, that the cat, not burglars, caused his bump. "But don't tell them, I'd be awfully embarrassed." In the confusion she does so anyway, and the ambulance attendants laugh so hard they drop the stretcher and break the man's arm.

When the reporter tried to verify the story, both the financier and the hospital to which he had allegedly been taken denied it. "Aha," reasoned the reporter, "a cover-up because of embarrassment." He printed it anyway, sans names. He did not know the same thing had happened a few months earlier at an American army base in Germany, with variants: a dog's cold nose, not the swipe of a cat's paw, caused a general, not a financier, to bust his head.

III.   The story reflects contemporary fears.

Four matrons from York, Pennsylvania, although apprehensive about crime, go to New York for a shopping trip.

Their husbands warn, "If someone wants your pocketbook or jewelry, don't put up a fight. Do what they ask." The women stay at the Plaza. As they ride the elevator to breakfast, a well-dressed black man with a Doberman pinscher gets on the elevator. "Sit," he commands. The women immediately sit on the floor.

At the lobby the man asks their room number. "Ten-sixteen," one of them blurts. He nods and walks away. The other women berate her. "Now we'll have to change rooms," they say. At the desk the clerk says, "Oh, you're the ladies from 1016. Mr. Reggie Jackson thought his dog might have frightened you; he would like to pick up your checks for breakfast." Robert Curvin, pursuing this yarn for *The New York Times* in January 1982, found that the same thing had happened to an old woman in The Bronx and in an office building in midtown Manhattan. He concluded it probably began with an old Bob Newhart story in which the man enters an elevator with a large white dog and commands, "Sit, Whitey," whereupon all other occupants drop to the floor.

IV.   An urban legend gains momentum from repetition in the press, even when used without names or other detail.

The dog-in-the-elevator story was on its way within days. *The Washington Post*'s "Ear" gossip column repeated it as gospel, even though the frightened York, Pennsylvania, matrons were journalistically transformed into two "mink-drenched" ladies from Washington. It was picked up in some form or other by newspapers, repeated on radio talk shows, and will, with Jackson's recent trade, live on, but the location of the story will now switch to Century City and Newport Beach. Jackson, of course, has firmly denied it, but who is he to stand in the way of a piece of urban folklore?

"Why are people so quick to believe it?" asked the *Times*'s Curvin. "Partly because it's a good story; more likely because it's the kind of story people need to believe. It offers relief from all the talk of crime, a way to laugh off fear. It ridicules racial stereotyping and urban paranoia."

V.   There is sometimes a grain of truth to the story which adds immeasurably to its persistence.

Almost any kid growing up in America after World War II has heard something on the order of the following:

Kid A: "I just heard about a Thunderbird that's for sale. It's less than a year old, loaded with all the extras, and has less than two thousand miles on it. You wanna know what they want for it?"

Kid B: "Jeez, I dunno, but I bet they want a lot."

Kid A: "All they want is fifty bucks for it."

Kid B: "You're crazy, there must be a catch."

Kid A: "Okay, here's the story. The guy who owned it got real depressed one night last spring and drove it into the woods where nobody could see him and he killed himself. He laid in the car all through the summer and wasn't discovered until fall. Now, they've tried everything, but they can't get the smell out of the car, so they want to unload it for fifty bucks."

Collectors of American folklore call this modern tale the "Death Car," and it exists in endless variations with the only constants being the cheapness of a fine car and the irremovable smell of death. The noted American folklorist Richard M. Dorson actually found a case of a real death car in a small town in Michigan. In his book *American Folklore*

Dorson asks, "Did this modern big-city legend originate with an actual incident in a hamlet of two hundred people in a rural Negro community and by the devious ways of folklore spread to Michigan's metropolises, and then to other states?" He answers, "Unlikely as it seems, the evidence from many variants, compared through the historical-geographical method of tracing folktales, calls for an affirmative answer."

VI.   Formal refutation does nothing to deter the popularity of a fable.

Because of his pro-German sentiments, H. L. Mencken ceased writing about politics and contemporary events during the First World War. Whiling away his time, he wrote a spurious history of the bathtub in America, published as "A Neglected Anniversary" in the New York *Evening Mail* on December 28, 1917. In greatly documented detail Mencken told how medical doctors denounced the bathtub as "an epicurean and obnoxious toy from England, designed to corrupt the democratic simplicity of the republic . . . dangerous to the health." (Among other "authorities," Mencken cited *The Western Medical Repository* of April 23, 1843.) He concluded that President Millard Fillmore installed the first White House bathtub in January 1851. The contractor was "Harper & Gillespie, a firm of Philadelphia engineers, who proposed to furnish a tub of cast iron, capable of floating the largest man." The implied presidential endorsement ended all objections to the bathtub, popular, medical, and otherwise, Mencken wrote.

First to Mencken's amusement, then to his consternation, serious scholars here and abroad accepted his "idle jocosities with complete seriousness." His article was cited in serious history and reference books, as well as in the press. He confessed the hoax in the *Chicago Tribune* on May 23, 1926, with some levity and the hope of burying the bogus history.

Alas, once falsehood gains a head start, truth puffs along to the rear.

The *Boston Herald,* on May 23 also, printed Mencken's "confession" on page seven of its editorial section, with a four-column headline and a two-column cartoon captioned "The American public will swallow anything." On June 13, three weeks later, the same editorial section reprinted the ten-year-old fake—"soberly and as a piece of news!" as Mencken declaimed in wonderment. He wrote a second disclaiming article for the *Tribune,* this one published on July 25, 1926. No matter, the myth raced on.

The "fact" that Fillmore installed the first presidential bathtub got into standard history books, and somehow with the first date of January 7, 1851 (Mencken had said only "early January"). TV comedian Johnny Carson used the "anniversary" for jokes twice in January 1966 on his opening monologue. A decade later three network television anchormen —Harry Reasoner, Roger Mudd, and John Chancellor—cited the "anniversary" on their evening newscasts. Incredibly, the hoax took in even such esteemed historians as Dr. Daniel J. Boorstin. In his *The Americans: The Democratic Experience,* published in 1973, Boorstin wrote, "In 1851, when President Millard Fillmore reputedly installed the first permanent bathtub and water closet in the White House, he was criticized for doing something that was 'both unsanitary and undemocratic.' "

P. J. Wingate, retired vice-president of the Du Pont Company, and a Mencken scholar, wrote a small book on the hoax and its aftermath (*H. L. Mencken's Un-neglected Anniversary,* published in 1980), plus articles in *The Washington Post, The Wall Street Journal, The Philadelphia Inquirer,* and elsewhere. "I had no more success in stopping the myth than did Mencken," lamented Wingate. "Serious scholars continue to use it." Indeed, the jacket of *Presidential Anecdotes,* by Dr. Paul F. Boller, Jr., published by the prestigious Oxford University Press in 1981, depicts a smiling Fillmore sitting in a bathtub, brandishing a cigar. In his text Boller (without citing a source) gives Mrs. Fillmore rather than her husband the credit: "She installed the first bathtub in the Executive Mansion (in the face of severe public criticism) and White House bathtubs have been a Presidential prerequisite ever since."

In researching this chapter the authors computed that American newspapers spent 113.7 years in the past three decades chasing down spurious urban myths. (See our earlier preliminary findings in *The Western Medical Repository*, April 23, 1981.) As a guide to the city editors of the nation, and their columnists, we submit herewith a further listing of hot stories that should be discarded as soon as they arrive at the office.

For the rest of you, however, who are not city editors, sit back and enjoy these gems of modern folklore. Novelist George V. Higgins, repeating the cement-truck story in the Boston *Globe,* makes the point: "Overlooked in the Calvinist approach, which determines the value of a true story solely by reference to the issue of whether it is in fact true, is a large category of stories for which the criterion of truth should be of no consequence whatsoever."

GREAT FABLES

THE ADMONISHING VOICE FROM HEAVEN

An employee of a Chicago radio station glances out his window and sees a couple embracing passionately in an office building across the street. He recognizes the man as an ad executive, and knows the woman is not his wife. He telephones the man's office, and after many rings he interrupts the lovemaking to answer. "This is God speaking," the radio employee says, "and I want you two sinners to stop that sort of conduct right now."

(In one early version the "voice from heaven" belonged to radio commentator Paul Harvey, who says that although he has heard and enjoyed the story, he has never been in a position to so speak. Other variants put the episode on a university campus in Boston and in a federal agency in Oklahoma City.)

THE BABY AND THE TURKEY

A baby-sitter waits until the parents have left and then takes LSD. Shortly thereafter she follows the instructions given to her: Put the turkey in the oven and put the baby to bed. She dutifully puts the baby in the oven and the turkey in bed.

BURYING GRANDMA

A family plans to spend its vacation in Canada on a canoe trip and decides to take Grandma, who is a spry eighty. After arriving at a remote river, the grandmother keels over dead. The local constable is notified, and he tells the family that the paperwork associated with recording the death and shipping the body out of the country is so great that they would be smarter if they just packed her up and made a beeline for the border. Taking this advice, the woman is wrapped in canvas and strapped into the canoe, which is tied to the roof of the family car. The family drives all day and at dark pulls into a motel near the U.S. border. They rise early to get a fresh start and find the car and canoe have been stolen.

(A common PS to this story is that the lady is never recovered and cannot be declared legally dead for a long time, therefore tying up her insurance. In Duncan Emrich's *Folklore on the American Land* there is another version in which the grandmother dies in the desert as the family drives to California.)

THE CAT AND THE SALMON

A woman cooks an elaborate salmon dish for a dinner party. Just before guests arrive, she finds her cat nibbling at the salmon. She tosses him out of the house and makes repairs with the sauce. The party goes well, and everyone leaves at midnight. While taking trash out, the woman finds the cat's corpse in the yard. Fearing her guests ate spoiled fish, she telephones them, and they rush to the hospital for stomach pumping, to their great discomfort and her great embarrassment. The woman's next-door neighbor phones the next morning. "I am awfully sorry. As I backed out of the driveway last night I ran over your cat. Not wishing to spoil your dinner party, I put his body over next to your house and decided to wait and tell you this morning."

THE CUT-RATE JAGUAR

"Nearly new Jaguar convertible for sale, low mileage, five hundred dollars cash." Would-be buyers were there at dawn; the first man in line handed over the money, then asked the woman selling the car, "Why is it so cheap? This car is easily worth ten thousand dollars."

"My husband ran away with his secretary to Las Vegas," the woman replied. "He went broke at the dice table the first night and wired me to sell the car and send him the money. He didn't say anything about price."

DADDY'S BOOTS

A man is bitten by a rattlesnake whose fangs penetrate his boot. The man dies from the bite. Years later the man's son, who was a baby at the time of his father's death, finds his father's boots and decides to try them on. He feels a sharp pain in one foot and later dies. It is discovered that one of the rattler's fangs had stuck in the boot and had still contained enough poison to claim the second member of the family.

THE LOVING BUT COLD HAND

The newlyweds, college students, are irked this winter morning when the car won't start. The husband says, "You walk on to class, I'll stay and tinker with the car." A few hours later she returns home and sees a pair of legs protruding from beneath the car, and hears someone working. She playfully scoops up a handful of snow, unzips the man's trousers, and gives him such a frigid surprise that his head hits the underside of the car with a clunk. She shakes him but cannot arouse him.

She runs inside to call an ambulance and finds her husband at his desk studying. "I couldn't do anything with the car," he says, "so the garage sent over a mechanic. He's working on it right now."

MANHATTAN WHITE

There is a mutant strain of unbelievably potent marijuana growing in the fecund New York sewer system. Because of the lack of light, it is white and hence known variously as "New York Albino," or "Manhattan White." The strain developed as a result of thousands of users flushing their stashes down toilets as narcs closed in.

(This is, of course, a variation of the belief that flushed alligators have flourished in the New York sewers.)

THE MANIAC'S HOOK

A young couple is parked in the local lovers' lane. Suddenly—as if struck with unexplained nervousness—the girl insists that she be taken home and the boy reluctantly agrees to leave. On the way home they turn on the car radio to hear that a one-armed homicidal maniac has just escaped from the local mental hospital. When they get to the girl's house, the boy gets out to open the door on the girl's side and finds the maniac's hook dangling from the door handle.

THE MATRON'S TV

A lady in a posh Manhattan apartment building opens her door to find a shabbily dressed man hauling off her neighbor's new color television. She asks him what he is doing, and he says that he is from a repair shop and is taking it off to be fixed. She asks the man if he could wait for a moment so that she could give him her set, which also needs fixing.

The man is, of course, a thief, and neither TV set is ever recovered.

THE NOTE FROM THE WITNESS

The woman, the victim in a rape trial, blushed when the prosecutor said, "Tell us what this man said to you when he first approached you." At her insistence the judge permitted her to write her reply on a piece of paper, which was passed to the jurors to read.

When a woman juror tried to give the paper to the man sitting next to her, he was dozing. She shook him awake. He read the note and flushed with embarrassment and hurriedly shoved it into his pocket.

"Mr. Bailiff," the judge called, "get that piece of paper from the juror and bring it here."

The juror replied in a panic, "No, sir, Your Honor, what that note says is a personal matter between this lady and me."

This episode has been related about most courthouses in the land, but as any veteran of trials will quickly note, it contains an inherent defect. The one witness whose testimony will not put a juror to sleep is the woman complainant in a rape case.

(This story not only gets told in courthouses but occasionally pops up in newspapers. Bill Gold of the *Washington Post* heard it so many times from readers of his column that he repeated it and then pointed out that it had all the earmarks of a fable. In his March 30, 1970, column, Gold says in part, "Some readers say the incident took place last week during a trial in Arlington, some say I'll find it in the records of a trial held a long time ago in Prince Georges County, one woman says she heard it from a woman who was on a jury and it happened in Washington, and a man says he had heard the story in California last year before moving here. So this one may have more miles on it than the other great 'true' story about the woman who drives away and leaves her husband stranded in his underdrawers after he has jumped out of the family trailer to find out the cause of a sudden stop.")

THE NOTE ON THE CAR

A man returns to a shopping-center parking lot to find his new car badly damaged and the following note stuck in the windshield: THE PEOPLE WHO SAW THIS HAPPEN AND WHO ARE NOW WATCHING ME THINK THAT I AM WRITING MY NAME AND ADDRESS AND THAT OF MY INSURANCE COMPANY ON THIS NOTE. I'M NOT.

THE PACKAGED CAT

An elderly woman's cat dies. At first she doesn't know what to do with it, since she lives in an apartment and there is no yard in which to bury it. She finally decides to wrap the dead cat in brown paper and take it downtown, where she will be able to leave it so that someone else can worry about burial. She first tries to leave it on the bus, but this doesn't work, as another passenger notices and catches up with her. This is repeated all day as others return the package. Defeated, she returns home and decides to open the package to have a final look at her beloved tabby. She unties the package and finds a leg of lamb.

THE PHANTOM HITCHHIKER

Two guys are on their way home from a party late one rainy night and they spot a very attractive young woman standing on a street corner without a raincoat or an umbrella. They offer her a ride, she hops in the back seat and gives them her address. One of the guys gives her his jacket because she looks so cold and wet. As they near her house, one of the guys turns around to double-check the address with her and is astonished to find that she has vanished. Dumbfounded, they decide to drive to the address that she had given them. They knock, and an older woman comes to the door. They begin telling her what has happened, and she interrupts.

"That was my daughter. She was killed on the corner where you picked her up. It happened two years ago on a night like this. She's done this several times since the accident."

The next morning the two young men verify the accident in the obituary file at the local paper. The obituary notes where she was buried and they decide to visit the grave. When they arrive they find the missing jacket draped over the tombstone.

(In his book *American Folklore* Richard Dorson reports that this story has been reported over a hundred times by folklorists. "It is found as far as Hawaii," he writes, "where a rickshaw supplants the auto, and is traced back to the nineteenth century, in America, Italy, Ireland, Turkey, and China with a horse and wagon picking up the benighted traveler.")

THE POODLE IN THE MICROWAVE

A woman bathes her pet poodle and, in a hurry to dry it, decides to pop the animal in her new microwave oven for a few seconds. The poodle explodes.

THE SECOND BLUE BOOK

The late folklorist Duncan Emrich, an academician himself, delighted in chasing down variants of an account of what he called "very clever trickery at final exam time at college." The standard tale (which professor Lew Girdler of San Jose State College, an Emrich contributor, dates to the 1930s at the University of California at Berkeley) goes as follows:

A student with an A average faces two essay questions on his final exam, the first of which completely stumps him. He jots random thoughts into his first blue book, then labels the second book "II" and begins with what appears to be the last sentence or so to the answer to the first essay question. Then he proceeds to answer the second essay question with brilliance. He turns in only the blue book marked "II."

A few days later the professor sends him a postcard notifying him of an A in the course, and apologizing for losing the first blue book.

There are other versions. The student cannot answer the first question, so he hands in a single page marked "2" and hides the other page in his notebook. Outside class he quickly looks up the answer to the first question and has a friend with a later class in the same room "find" the first page on the floor and hand it to the teacher. In still another version, the student writes a letter to his mother in the blue book, saying he finished the exam early, and is killing time, and what a fine fellow the professor is. He hands in the blue book with the letter, hurriedly does the exam out of class, and mails the second blue book to his mother. When the instructor calls him to inquire why he handed in a letter rather than the exam, he explains he must have crossed the two books, and that he will have his mother mail back the other book, without opening the envelope.

As Professor Emrich stated, "Such deception of innocent professors is greatly to be deplored, and the ingenuity of students equally to be admired."

THE SEVERED HAND I

Several frisky medical students plan to play a trick on a nurse. They tie the severed hand from one of their laboratory cadavers to the light string in a supply room that the nurse uses. The nurse goes into the room but does not come out for a long time. One of the med students becomes impatient, walks in, and finds the light on and the nurse sitting on the floor. Her hair has turned white and she is nibbling on the hand.

SEVERED HAND II

A male medical student who commuted each day along a stretch of the Massachusetts Turnpike was trying to come up with a way to attract the attention of a sexy toll booth attendant. He hit on the idea of taking a hand from his cadaver, attaching a quarter to the palm, and giving it to the lady in the booth. He decided to go ahead with the grisly gag, and the woman dropped dead of shock.

THE SKI ACCIDENT

A woman takes a lift to the top of a ski slope, where she finds she has to relieve herself. She removes her skis, heads off behind a tree, and pulls her pants down. She accidentally lets go of her skis, which start down the mountain. With her pants down around her ankles, she lunges forward to grab the skis. Not only does she miss them, but slips and starts sliding down the mountain on her bare backside. In this manner she goes all the way to the bottom.

Later she is in the emergency room of·the local hospital having her scrapes and bruises attended to and a man comes in. The emergency-room staff is surprised to see this man, as he is reputed to be the best skier on the mountain. It is obvious that he has dislocated his shoulder.

"How did you do that?" asked one of the nurses.

"Well, I was going up the lift and happened to look down and saw something go by that was so unbelievable that I pulled my shoulder out when I turned around to see if it was real."

"What was it?"

"If I told you, you wouldn't believe me."

THE STRANGE GAS STATION ATTENDANT

A young woman must return home from college in the middle of the night because of a sudden illness in her family. Her nervousness increases after she pulls into a filling station because the attendant keeps looking at her in an odd manner. After he pumps the gas, he insists that she get out of the car. She resists, but he finally convinces her to get out and see because it could be a "major problem with the car." As she gets out, he grabs her, pushes her into the gas station office, and locks the door behind them. As she opens her mouth to scream, he says calmly, "I'm sorry I had to do that, but there's a man lying on the back seat of the car with a knife."

(In one version of this popular college tale, the coed and the man at the gas station fall in love and get married.)

MENCKEN'S X-RATED CREDOS: Special Appendix I

When Mencken and Nathan finished *The American Credo* they put together a private collection of credos that were presumably too outrageous to appear in a book in 1920. The authors had their blue appendix privately published and distributed it to friends as a Christmas gift. Thanks to the Mencken Room at the Enoch Pratt Free Library in Baltimore, we have obtained a copy of the Christmas appendix. A sampling:

- That all floozies wear red neckties and colored handkerchiefs.
- That the couch in a theatrical manager's office is used at least twenty times a day.
- That toilet paper is quite unknown in the country, and all yokels use corncobs instead.
- That if a city man with a fresh shoeshine walks across a meadow he invariably steps into several large cowflops.
- That piles are caused by sitting on cold stone steps.
- That all United States senators have difficulty passing their water.

•   That whenever the Elks hold a convention the whore-madams of the town bring in extra talent from five hundred miles around.

•   That the dashboard of a country beau's buggy always bears the marks of his footprints upside down.

•   That whenever a woman guest, fashionably dressed, takes the baby of the house in her lap, the baby pees.

A CHECKLIST FOR CRITICS:
Special Appendix II

H. L. Mencken was perhaps one of the few serious writers who delight in reading savage reviews of their work, and the more biting the commentary, the more he howled with glee. (Indeed, Mencken even published a short compilation of the more picturesque billingsgate directed at him in print, *Menckeniana: A Schimpflexikon*, Alfred A. Knopf, 1927.) Mencken carefully (perhaps even joyfully) clipped reviews of *The American Credo* and pasted them into his scrapbooks, which now adorn the Mencken Room of the Enoch Pratt Free Library in Baltimore. A sampling of what critics wrote of this predecessor volume to our own modest work:

> The linguistic coat is brilliant and vari-colored, but this observation leads one on a converging trail of natural history. There is an animal of brilliant coat classified as an American *mephitine musteloid carnivore*, whose glands secrete a liquid of very offensive odor which can be ejected at will. But this animal doesn't trail in pairs, as a rule, and it doesn't become offensive unless some intruder crowds it.
>
> —*The Dallas Morning News*

The writers apparently would have had as much fun at their volumes as would a couple of naughty children who stand up and ask awkward questions in Sunday school, but apparently they got so "het-up" that they became absolutely serious, which is always unfortunate for a critic. He then is apt to be both carried away and "put away" by those he criticizes.

—The Philadelphia *North American*

Little that is sacred to Americans escapes. Basing argument upon assertion that the man who is moral can never be honest, that morality and honesty have nothing in common, the authors . . . spew right and left at laws, courts, institutions, authorities, professors, judges, uplifters, reformers . . .

—*The News and Courier* (Charleston, S.C.)

It has been written with brains. It is a calm, careful, cautious, ably drawn, full-length portrait of America in all her boobery. . . . Rare as such an outcome may seem, there is some possibility that it may set someone thinking. . . .

—*The Baltimore Sun*

THANKS

A number of stalwart credo collectors have contributed their own findings to this work, and we thank them for their generosity. The discoveries of the following people, often in their own words, are spread throughout the book:

John Anders
Ryan Anthony
Harriet and
    David Bernstein
Art Berwick
Walter Blair
Murray Teigh Bloom
Richard Cheyney
Nonnee Coan
Bob Cochran
Mark B. Cohen
Virginia Cressey
James J. Crowe
James Davis
Nancy Dickson

Rose DeWolf
Lynn Eden
R.K. Edson
Wayne C. Fields, Jr.
Marguerite Foster
Jim Goulden
A. C. Greene
Jim Hely
Charles Holmes
Terri Hundley
Michael G. Hutsko
Joan C. Kaye
Bill Kelly
Don King
William M. Kipp

Erwin Knoll
Gary M. Knowlton
Martin S. Kottmeyer
Lois Landis Kurowski
Arthur H. Lewis
Pete McAlevey
J. Marshall Magner
Maurice Marsolais
Paula Matzek
Robert Norrish
Andrew J. Novotney, S.J.
Judith Podell
Frank S. Preston
Dan Rapoport
Ken Rigsbee

R. J. Shipley
Bob Skole
Larry M. Slavens
Leslie Cantrell Smith
Robert D. Specht
Bill Tammeus
Craig Tovey
James Tovey
Elaine Viets
Jerry Wall
Greg Walter
Rozanne Weissman
John Edward Weems
P. J. Wingate

BIBLIOGRAPHY

Allport, Gordon W., and Postman, Leo. *The Psychology of Rumor.* New York: Henry Holt and Company, 1947.

Anders, John. "We Hold These Truths to Be Self-evident Bromides." *The Dallas Morning News,* June 12, 1979.

Baker, Ronald L. "The Influence of Mass Culture on Modern Legends." *Southern Folklore Quarterly* 40 (1979), pp. 367–376.

Barry, Edward. "A Word to the Wise: What You 'Know' Can Hurt You, Too." *Chicago Tribune,* December 20, 1960.

Bennett, William J. "Simple Truths." *Newsweek,* January 7, 1980.

Blair, Walter, and Hill, Hamlin. *America's Humor: From Poor Richard to Doonesbury.* Oxford University Press, New York, 1978.

Boller, Paul F., Jr. *Presidential Anecdotes.* New York: Oxford University Press, 1981.

Brunvand, Jan Harold. *The Study of American Folklore: An Introduction.* New York: Norton, 1968.

Burnam, Tom. *The Dictionary of Misinformation.* New York: Thomas Y. Crowell Co., 1975.

————. *More Misinformation.* New York: Lippincott and Crowell, 1980.

Caldwell, Otis W., and Lundeen, Gerhard E. *Do You Believe It? Curious Habits and Strange Beliefs of Civilized Man.* Garden City: Garden City Publishing Co., Inc., 1937.

Camp, John. *Magic, Myth and Medicine.* New York: Taplinger, 1973.

Chase, Stuart. *American Credos*. New York: Harper and Brothers, 1962.

Chaundler, Christine. *Every Man's Book of Superstitions*. New York: Philosophical Library, 1970.

Coffin, Tristram Potter. *A Proper Book of Sexual Folklore*. New York: Seabury Press, 1978.

Curvin, Robert. "Sit!" *The New York Times*, January 7, 1982.

Daley, Robert. *World Beneath the City*. Philadelphia: Lippincott, 1959.

DeWolf, Rose. "Would You Believe Some of the Things We Believe?" *The Bulletin* (Philadelphia), April 30, 1980.

Dorson, Richard M. *American Folklore*. Chicago: The University of Chicago Press, 1959.

———. *America in Legend*. New York: Pantheon, 1973.

———. *Land of the Millrats*. Cambridge: Harvard University Press, 1981.

Ellul, Jacques. *A Critique of the New Commonplaces*. New York: Alfred A. Knopf 1968.

Emrich, Duncan. *Folklore on the American Land*. Boston: Little, Brown, 1972.

Evans, Bergen. *The Natural History of Nonsense*. New York: Alfred A. Knopf, 1953.

———. *A Spoor of Spooks*. New York: Alfred A. Knopf, 1954.

Ferm, Vergilius. *A Brief Dictionary of American Superstitions*. New York: Philosophical Library, 1965.

Flaubert, Gustave. *The Dictionary of Accepted Ideas*, (trans. and with an introduction by Jacques Barzun). New York: New Directions, 1954.

Fowler, Will. *The Second Handshake*. Secaucus, N.J.: Lyle Stuart, Inc., 1980.

Gillins, Peter. "Have You Heard About the Mouse in the Pop Bottle?" UPI story which appeared in the *Montgomery Journal*, February 3, 1982.

Gold, Bill. "The District Line." *The Washington Post*, March 30, 1979.

Groner, Jonathan. "The Neatness of Myths." *The Washington Post*, April 1, 1979.

Haas, Alan D. "Rumors." *Sunday World-Herald Magazine of the Midlands*, August 17, 1980.

Hering, Daniel W. *Foibles and Fallacies of Science*. New York: Van Nostrand, 1924.

Higgins, George W. "A Little Fantasy for Your Health." Boston *Globe*, August 19, 1981.

Hobson, Thayer. *Morrow's Almanack and Every-Day-Book for 1930*. New York: William Morrow and Co., 1929.

Knapp, Mary and Herbert. *One Potato, Two Potato . . . The Secret Education of American Children*. New York: Norton, 1976.

Lapham, Lewis H. "Program Notes." *Harper's*, May, 1979.

Leccese, Michael. "Looking for Mr. Dillinger." The *Washington Tribune,* April 1980.

Mansfield, Stephanie. "The Man in the Moon." *The Washington Post,* January 23, 1982.

Molleson, John. "The Explosive Power of Rumors." *Parade,* May 19, 1968.

Montagu, Ashley, and Darling, Edward. *The Ignorance of Certainty.* New York: Harper and Row, 1970.

———, and Darling, Edward. *The Prevalence of Nonsense.* New York: Harper and Row, 1967.

Morris, Scot. "Psssssst! Have you heard . . . ?" *OMNI.* July 1981.

Nathan, George Jean. *American Credo.* New York: Blue Ribbon Books, 1927.

———, and Mencken, H. L.. *The American Credo.* New York: Alfred A. Knopf, 1920.

Oberg, James. "Spaceflight Folklore." *Analog,* September 1980.

Opie, Iona and Peter. *The Lore and Language of Schoolchildren.* Oxford: Oxford Press, 1959.

Palmer, Barbara. "Myths of Washington." *The Washingtonian,* January 1980.

"Proctor & Gamble Is Clean." *Newsweek,* April 7, 1980.

Runes, Dagoburt D. *Dictionary of Thought.* New York: Philosophical Library, 1959.

Sarnoff, Jane, and Ruffins, Reynold. *Take Warning! A Book of Superstitions.* New York: Scribners, 1978.

"The Great Fables of Our Time." *Oui,* September 1976.

"The Hell with the Donuts." *The DAV Magazine.* April, 1961.

Viets, Elaine. "If There's One Thing for Certain, It's That . . ." *St. Louis Post-Dispatch,* July 1, 1979.

Ward, Philip. *Dictionary of Common Fallacies.* New York: Oleander Press, 1978.

Weinstein, Jeff. "Four Lies about Gay Male Fashion." *The Village Voice,* April 8–14, 1981.

Werwein, Austin C. "Logo Rumors Haunt P&G." *The Washington Post,* March 26, 1980.

West, Woody. "How the Public Was Snake-Bitten by a Rumor." *Washington Star,* February 23, 1969.

Wiggam, Albert Edward. *The Marks of a Clear Mind.* New York: Blue Ribbon Books, Inc., 1931.

Wingate, P. J.. *H. L. Mencken's Un-Neglected Anniversary.* Hockessin, Delaware: The Holly Press, 1980.

INDEX

Happiness, 69, 70
Harding, Warren G., 30
Harrison, William Henry, 30
Harvard Business School, 35
Harvey, Paul, 75, 113, 137
Hats, wearing inside, 59
Headaches, 59
Health and medicine, 57–61, 92
Heart, the, 68
Hefner, Hugh, 75–76
Height, 62, 94; children's growth, 19
Heinz company, 16
Hemorrhoids (piles), 149
Hess, Rudolf, 38
Hiccuping, 59, 61
Higgins, George V., 136
Highballs, 33
High Noon, 113
High school, 108
Hill, Hamlin, xv
Historic credos, 62–67
Hitchhiker, phantom, 144
Hitler, Adolf, 38
H. L. Mencken's Un-neglected Anniversary, 135
Hogs, 103
Holbrook, Hal, xviii
Holidays, 105
Homosexuality, 83–85
Honey, 92
Hook, Maniac's, 141
Hoover, Herbert, 38, 100
Hoover, J. Edgar, 38, 56
Hope diamond, 64
Horses, riding, 83
Horseshoes, 121, 122

Hot dogs, 48, 49
Houses, building, 56
Hughes, Howard, 38
Human condition, the, 68–70
Humor, sense of, 73
Hunters, 42
Hypnosis, 104

Ice cream, 50, 51
Illiteracy, 108
Indian Ocean, 86
Infamy!, 66
Inflation, 14
Inns, 106
Insects, 125
Intelligence, 17, 19, 88, 94; genius, 69; and nervous breakdowns, 104; women and, 82
Iowans, 22, 23
Iran, 66
Irish (Irishmen), 77, 89
Italy (Italians), 64, 77

Jackson, Reggie, 132, 133
Jaffe, Harry Joe, 76
Janssen, David, 38